DON
Canto

CW00346275

ROUTLEDGE ENGLISH TEXTS

GENERAL EDITOR: T. S. Dorsch, M.A. (Oxon)
Professor of English at the University
of Durham

DON JUAN

Cantos I–IV

(*Abridged*)

LORD BYRON

EDITED BY T. S. DORSCH

LONDON

ROUTLEDGE & KEGAN PAUL

Published 1967
by Routledge & Kegan Paul Ltd
Broadway House, 68–74 Carter Lane
London, EC4V 5EL

Second impression 1968
Third impression 1969
Fourth impression 1971
Fifth impression 1973

Printed in Great Britain
by Richard Clay (The Chaucer Press) Ltd
Bungay, Suffolk

ISBN 0 7100 4516 6 (p)
ISBN 0 7100 4515 8 (c)

SERIES EDITOR'S PREFACE

THE ROUTLEDGE ENGLISH TEXTS are designed primarily for the use of sixth-form pupils and undergraduates. Each volume is edited by a scholar who is an authority on the period which it represents and who has also had experience of teaching and examining at the school-leaving or the undergraduate level. The aim is to provide, in the introductions and notes, both sufficient explanatory material to enable the texts to be read with full understanding, and critical commentary of a kind that will stimulate thought and discussion.

The series will include both single works of some length and collections of shorter works. Where a work is too long to fit within the limits of size necessarily laid down for a text-book series—such a work, for example as *The Prelude*, or *Don Juan* —it will normally be represented by a single extended extract of several consecutive books or cantos rather than by an abridgement of the whole, since an abridgement runs the risk of losing the cumulative effects that are important in a work of some scope. In the anthologies a few authors of a particular period will be well represented, in the belief that a reasonably thorough study of a limited field is more profitable than a superficial study of a wide field, and that a more than passing acquaintance with an author is of value in itself.

T. S. DORSCH

CONTENTS

PREFACE

Byron's *Don Juan* cannot be fully appreciated unless it is read in long stretches; it derives much of its highly individual flavour from its abrupt transitions in subject and mood, from the jostling together of the serious and the comic, the pathetic and the ribald, the beautiful and the grotesque, the sublime and the satirical. I have, therefore, in this selection, presented two complete episodes in Juan's career, or three, if we may count as an episode the adventures by sea which take place between the Juan–Julia *fabliau* of Canto I and the island-idyll of Juan and Haidée. The selection comprises the first three cantos of the poem and about three-quarters of the fourth; it ends with the death of Haidée.

However, some slight abridgement has been necessary, although I have undertaken it with reluctance. My aim has been to preserve the heterogeneous character of the poem. I have therefore omitted no complete sections, however self-contained they appear to be, and very few of the digressions which are so essential an element of the work. Stanzas have been omitted only where their omission does not seriously affect the spirit or the proportions of the passages in which they occur. For example, the account of Juan's adolescent musings in Canto I has been slightly shortened, and in Canto II some details have been left out of the description of the storm and of the drifting in the long-boat. I have not bowdlerised. All omissions have been recorded in the notes, with summaries of the omitted material.

T. S. D.

INTRODUCTION

I

LIFE OF BYRON

Much more has been written about Lord Byron's life and personality than about his poetry. Yet in the *genre* which he made peculiarly his own in the last half-dozen years of his life, the comic verse satire, he is supreme among English poets, and indeed the poetry that he wrote during these years gives him claims to be ranked among the great poets of Europe. It is not difficult to see why the attention of scholars has been concentrated on the man rather than the poet. Byron himself did much to foster, or did little to discourage, the growth of the Byron Legend—the legend of the aristocrat who tossed off poetry as a diversion proper to a man of his station, the wronged victim of a hypocritical society, the man of contradictory moods and passions, ardent and romantic, gloomy and disillusioned, or, as Macaulay expresses it, 'proud, moody, cynical, with defiance on his brow, and misery in his heart, a scorner of his kind, implacable in revenge, yet capable of deep and strong affection'. Moreover, to a greater degree than most poets, he drew directly upon the circumstances of his own life and his ever-changing impressions and feelings for the material of his poetry, and more than any other English poet he has been identified with the heroes of his poems—with Childe Harold, the romantic pilgrim, with Lara, 'a stranger in this breathing world, An erring spirit from another hurl'd', with Manfred, the outcast, with Juan, the ardent lover. Clearly some knowledge of Byron's life is necessary for a full understanding of his poetry, although it must never be forgotten that his standing as a poet depends on the poetic effects of which he shows himself capable rather than on the autobiographical interest of his poems.

George Gordon Noel Byron, sixth Baron, was born in London in 1788, the son of 'Mad Jack' Byron, a dissolute officer in the Guards who died when the boy was three years old, and Catherine Gordon of Gight, a woman of irascible temper with whom he quarrelled a great deal. He suffered much from the medical maltreatment of the deformed foot with which he was born. His early years were spent in Aberdeen, where he attended the Grammar School, until, at the age of ten, he succeeded to the title on the death of his great-uncle, the 'wicked' Lord Byron, and went to live at Newstead Abbey, near Nottingham. His ancestry, his upbringing, and his sensitivity about his physical disability all no doubt contributed to his later instability of character—although the extent of this instability has probably been exaggerated.

Byron continued his education at Harrow, where he represented the school at cricket against Eton, having someone to run for him, and in 1805 he went up to Trinity College, Cambridge, where he led a somewhat dissipated life—among other irregularities, he kept a bear—and fell heavily into debt; he also rode, shot, and boxed, and became a very fine swimmer. In 1807 he published *Hours of Idleness*, a much revised edition of two previous collections of poems that he had written as a schoolboy and undergraduate. The volume received some favourable reviews, but was lashed by Brougham (not Jeffrey, as Byron believed) in the *Edinburgh Review*. 'I recollect the effect on me of the Edinburgh on my first poem,' Byron wrote to Shelley some years later; 'it was rage and resistance and redress; but not despondency nor despair.' The redress took the form of *English Bards, and Scotch Reviewers* (1809), a satire in couplets in the manner of Pope, 'the little Queen Anne's man', whom Byron admired all his life. The poem has little of Pope's wit and polish, and is memorable chiefly for some amusing couplets on Southey, Wordsworth, and Coleridge, the first of many attacks on these poets.

On leaving Cambridge, Byron travelled abroad for nearly two years with his friend John Cam Hobhouse, visiting Spain, Portugal, Greece, and Turkey, and on his return took his seat in the House of Lords. In 1812 appeared the poetic fruits of the Mediterranean journey, the first two cantos of *Childe Harold's Pilgrimage*. This was an immediate success; in Byron's own words, he 'awoke to find himself famous'. During the next three or four years he published the narrative poems which, with their 'Byronic' heroes, confirmed his position as the most popular poet of the day—*The Giaour, The Bride of Abydos, The Corsair, Lara, Parisina*, and *The Siege of Corinth*. During these years, too, he was much sought after in London society, and had a number of love-affairs, more often as the pursued than the pursuer; his affair with Lady Caroline Lamb, who threw herself at his head, became a public scandal. In 1815 he married Anne Isabella Milbanke, whose intellectual interests provided material for the satirical portrait of Donna Inez in *Don Juan*. The marriage, of which a daughter, Augusta Ada, was born, lasted only a year, when Lady Byron obtained a separation on the grounds of her husband's cruelty and insanity; at the same time there were sinister whispers that Byron had been carrying on an incestuous relationship with his half-sister, Augusta Leigh. He found himself ostracised by the society by which he had previously been lionised, and in April 1816, disgusted by what he regarded as the hypocrisy and humbug of his countrymen, he left England, never to return.

Byron now travelled through Belgium and Germany to Switzerland, where he met Shelley and Mary Godwin, whom Shelley married after the death of his first wife at the end of 1816. The two poets became friends; they later saw a good deal of each other in Italy. Here too Byron had a liaison with Mary's stepsister, Jane Clairmont; their daughter, Allegra, lived only a few years. Moving on to Italy, Byron spent most of his time in the next few years at Venice, where he kept a menagerie of strange animals, and had a number of love-affairs; the longest of these, lasting for several years, was with the Countess Teresa Guiccioli, whose husband apparently did not object to sharing a house with the lovers. Meanwhile he had been writing the third and fourth cantos of *Childe Harold* (published in 1816 and 1818), which are poetically far more mature and interesting than Cantos I and II. To this period belong also, among other writings, the verse dramas by which Byron himself set so much store—*Manfred, Marino Faliero, Sardanapalus, The Two Foscari*, and *Cain*, the last of which offended many readers by its attitude towards sin.

With *Beppo*, a narrative poem in *ottava rima* published in 1818, Byron found his true vocation as a poet, and entered upon the period of his greatest poetry. Based on an anecdote which Byron heard in Venice, *Beppo* is an amusing story of a

wife–husband–lover relationship in Venetian high life into
which Byron introduces good-humoured satire of the moral
and social conventions of his day—'it has politics and ferocity,'
said Byron; its spirit is not unlike that of Chaucer's *fabliaux*,
and in its discursive manner of narration, too, and its many
digressions, it is reminiscent of Chaucer's way of telling a
story, as is much of *Don Juan*. *Beppo* is important in Byron's
artistic development for the new tone and new techniques that
it brought into his poetry. With his increasing self-knowledge
and emotional maturity, he was now able to treat with laughter
and urbane mockery what in *Childe Harold* and his other early
poems he had seen as cause for bitterness and self-pity.

Four months after the publication of *Beppo*, Byron wrote to
his friend Thomas Moore, the poet, that he had finished the
first canto of a poem 'in the style and manner of *Beppo*', and
that it was called *Don Juan*; the growth of this poem in the
course of the next six years is described in a later section. In
1822 appeared *The Vision of Judgment*, a travesty of Southey's
poem of the same name, which was a eulogy of George III,
and in the Preface to which Southey attacked Byron and his
works; Byron's reply contains some powerful satire both of
Southey and of the late king. Other poems written in these last
years include *The Island* (1823), a beautiful romantic verse
narrative based on the mutiny of the Bounty.

Byron was at all times a strong advocate of liberty, both
personal and national, and he liked to think of himself as being
essentially a man of action. In 1823 he was invited to join the
Greek revolutionary committee which was working for the
liberation of Greece from Turkish rule. He threw himself with
fervour into the cause, working strenuously to reconcile
differences between the Greek leaders, and showing excellent
powers of organisation. Had he lived longer, he might well have
led the Greeks to victory, and it is at least possible that he
might have been offered the Greek throne. However, in April
1824 he contracted a fever, and died at his headquarters at
Missolonghi, deeply mourned by his friends, both English and
Greek. By the Greeks he is still honoured as a national hero.
His body was brought back to England in a warship; refused
burial in Westminster Abbey on moral grounds, it was laid in
the family vault at Hucknall Torkard, in Nottinghamshire.

The relevance of Byron's biography to a full appreciation of his poetry becomes especially apparent in the reading of *Don Juan*, and the notes in the present volume contain many references to the facts of his life.

2

THE LITERARY BACKGROUND OF *DON JUAN*

The origins of the Don Juan legend are obscure, though certain elements have their roots in folklore. As a literary figure Don Juan, whose name in English means simply Sir John, was created by the early seventeenth-century Spanish playwright Gabriel Téllez (1571–1641), who is better known under his pseudonym of Tirso de Molina. Tirso's play, entitled *El Burlador de Sevilla y convidada de piedra* (*The Jester of Seville and the Stone Guest*), was probably written in about 1616; it first appeared under his name in a collection of works by Lope de Vega and other authors which was published in 1630. Byron appears to have known this play, and certainly knew other dramatic versions based on it; and since Tirso's form of the legend provided at least the starting-point for his poetic *Don Juan*, some account of it must be given.

The hero of the play is Don Juan Tenorio, son of a nobleman of Seville. On a visit to the Neapolitan court, he gains access by night to the bedroom in the royal palace of the Duchess Isabela. He is disguised as the Duke Octavio, to whom she is betrothed. As he is leaving, she discovers the deception, and raises the alarm. Juan escapes with the connivance of his uncle, who is the Spanish Ambassador at the court. Out of shame the Duchess declares that it is the Duke Octavio who has shared her bed, and the King orders the arrest of the pair; Octavio escapes, however, and flees from Naples. Journeying home to Seville, Juan is shipwrecked on the Spanish coast; he manages to swim ashore, and is tended by a beautiful fisher-girl, Tisbea, who falls in love with him. He promises to marry her, spends a night with her, and then returns to Seville.

At the court of King Alfonso of Castile, Juan meets Octavio, who has taken refuge there, and who does not know that he is the deceiver of Isabela. King Alfonso knows this, however, and that justice may be done, he decrees that Juan shall marry Isabela as soon as she can be brought from Naples, and that in

the meantime he shall be banished to Lebrija; as consolation
for his loss, Octavio is promised the hand of Donna Ana,
daughter of the Commander of the Order of Calatrava—who,
however, is in love with the Marquis de Mota. On the eve of
his banishment Juan disguises himself as the Marquis, and
enters Ana's bedchamber; she sees through the deception and
raises an outcry, and Juan kills her father, who comes to her
help. The Marquis is arrested for the murder.

On his way to Lebrija, Juan comes upon a rustic wedding,
and contrives to seduce the bride, and then for some reason
returns to Seville, where he learns that the Duke and the
Marquis now know him for the author of the crimes for which
they have been held responsible, and that Isabela and Tisbea
are also on his tracks. Vengeance is also threatened in an
inscription beneath a statue that has been set up of Ana's
father, the Commander. Juan enters the chapel where the
statue stands, defies the threat, and, devil-may-care as ever,
invites the statue to sup with him. This the statue does, and
exacts from Juan a promise to be its guest at a banquet in the
chapel on the following night. Juan keeps the engagement,
when the statue takes him by the hand and hurls him down to
hell. His servant reports to the King what has happened, and
with Juan's death there remain no impediments to the marriages of Isabela and Octavio and Ana and the Marquis.

This plot is the basis of innumerable literary treatments of
the Don Juan story in a variety of languages; in a recent study
Leo Weinstein catalogues nearly 500 versions, representing
almost every European and American country.[1] A very large
number of them have been written for the theatre. For
example, to name only well-known versions, to the same
century as Tirso's *El Burlador* belong Molière's *Dom Juan, ou
Le Festin de Pierre* (1665) and Thomas Shadwell's *The Libertine* (1676); also in this century, Juan provided plots for the
commedia dell' arte, and in the following century for the
German puppet theatre. Musical versions also appeared;
indeed, the best-known of all Juans is surely the Don Giovanni
of Mozart's beautiful opera (1787), for which Lorenzo Da
Ponte wrote the libretto. There were two other Don Juan
operas in the same year as Mozart's. More than a century
earlier Henry Purcell had composed some music for Shadwell's
play, and Gluck wrote a Don Juan ballet in 1758. In the early

nineteenth century Juan became a popular figure on the London stage as the hero of pantomimes (Byron refers to one of these), farces, comic operas, and the like; of these debased versions one of the most successful was William T. Moncrieff's *Giovanni in London, or The Libertine Reclaimed* (1817). Byron could confidently, at the beginning of his poem, speak of 'our ancient friend Don Juan'. Among recent dramatic handlings of Juan are those of Bernard Shaw in *Man and Superman* (1903), which, however, has little connexion with the legend in its classical form, of Edmond Rostand in *La Dernière nuit de Don Juan* (1921), of Henry de Montherlant in *Don Juan* (1956), and of Max Frisch in *Don Juan oder die Liebe zur Geometrie* (1962).[2] Of English poems embodying the legend, Browning's *Fifine at the Fair* is, after Byron's *Don Juan*, the most well-known.

Juan has undergone many transformations in the course of the centuries. Each author has refashioned him according to his tastes and preoccupations or the spirit of his age, and he has appeared sometimes as hero, sometimes as villain, sometimes as gentleman, sometimes as scoundrel, sometimes as mere voluptuary, sometimes as thinker. Most of the authors, however, have retained at least some features of Tirso de Molina's plot, and of the character of the cynical and heartless lover that he gave to his hero. Byron's treatment is out of the ordinary. His Juan is shown as a lover, and it is possible that he owes to the early form of the legend the idea of the shipwreck and the seashore and island idyll of his Juan and Haidée; but everything else appears to be his own, based on his own experience and observation, or on reading that has nothing to do with the legend. Moreover, he is writing a long, rambling narrative poem, and is able to devise for his hero more and more diverse love-affairs than would be possible in a play. His treatment of these love-affairs is discussed later; all that need be said here is that none of them is similar in character to those of the traditional Don Juan.

For particular episodes Byron drew on a very wide range of reading. This is also considered later. Where specific 'sources' can be identified, attention is drawn to them in the notes.

Byron wrote *Beppo* in the autumn of 1817, at the same time as he was making his final revisions and additions to Canto IV of *Childe Harold*. In October that year, referring to *Beppo*, he

B

informed his publisher, John Murray, that he had written a poem which was 'humourous, in or after the excellent manner of Mr. Whistlecraft (whom I take to be Frere), on a Venetian anecdote which amused me'. Here Byron acknowledges his debt to John Hookham Frere for the manner and spirit of *Beppo*, which were to be the predominant manner and spirit also of *Don Juan*—colloquial, witty, comic, mocking, although this manner, as will appear, is often a mask for what is serious in intention. Frere, among other things a notable translator of Aristophanes, was one of the most accomplished writers of burlesque of his day; the early cantos of his *Prospectus and Specimen of an Intended National Work*, a mock-romantic Arthurian poem in the Italian *ottava rima* stanza, published under the *noms de plume* of William and Robert Whistlecraft, appeared in 1817. Byron was familiar also with the Italian burlesque poets who were Frere's models; indeed, while conscious of what he owed directly to Frere, he declared of *Beppo* that 'Berni is the origin of *all*'. Francesco Berni, an Italian poet of the early sixteenth century, is best known for his jocular and satirical poems, *Rime giocosi*, and for his revision of Boiardo's *Orlando Innamorato*; it was his tone and his easy familiarity of style that Frere and Byron adopted, not his verse form, which was derived from Dante's *terza rima*. However, for the amoral flippancy of *Beppo*, its apparent form-lessness, and its satire of current political and social outlooks, Byron also owed much to the *Novelle galanti* (in *ottava rima*) and *Gli animali parlanti* (a mocking political fable is *sesta rima*) of another Italian burlesque poet, Giambattista Casti (1724–1803). And before he had proceeded far with the composition of *Don Juan*, he read the *Morgante maggiore* of Luigi Pulci ('sire of the half-serious rhyme'—1432–84), which he was later to translate. This fine *ottava rima* poem is notable, among other reasons, for its racy manner, and for its admirable comedy and burlesque.

It should be apparent by now that *Don Juan* owes more to the Italian burlesque poets than to Tirso de Molina's Don Juan play and its derivatives, and even to the Italians it owes almost nothing of its content; it remains Byron's own creation.

3

THE COMPOSITION OF *DON JUAN*

Byron began *Don Juan* at the beginning of July 1818. In September he wrote to Thomas Moore: 'I have finished the first canto (a long one, of about 180 octaves) of a poem in the style and manner of *Beppo*, encouraged by the good success of the same. It is called *Don Juan*, and is meant to be a little quietly facetious upon everything. But I doubt whether it is not—at least as far as it has yet gone—too free for these very modest days.' At first Byron was diffident about the merits of his poem; but by January 1819 he had come to realise how good it was, and in October that year, when the first two cantos had been published and Canto III was well advanced, he wrote to his friend Douglas Kinnaird: 'As to "Don Juan", confess, confess, you dog, and be candid, that it is the sublime of *that there* sort of writing.'

After much revision, and with some additions, Canto I was taken to London by Lord Lauderdale in November 1818. John Murray and his advisers were unwilling to take the responsibility of publishing a work which they knew would give offence, and on the whole Byron's friends agreed with them; but Byron was determined to see his poem in print, and entered upon an increasingly acrimonious correspondence with Murray, in the course of which he sent him further revisions and additions, including a draft of the dedication to Southey, which, however, he agreed to suppress, since the publication was to be anonymous. It is still sometimes maintained that Byron dashed off his poetry hastily and carelessly—perhaps late at night after a party, or on returning from a ride—and that he was indifferent both to its many imperfections and to its reception by the public, and he himself encouraged the impression that he regarded it merely as a diversion that filled the idle moments of the life of a nobleman; he was, in fact, a careful and conscientious craftsman, a 'professional' poet, and although he must have composed quickly and easily in the first place, he polished and repolished what he wrote, as indeed a glance at the Variorum edition of *Don Juan* will make clear. While he was revising Canto I, he was working busily on Canto II. Eventually he had his way with Murray, and Cantos I and

II appeared on 15 July 1819. The early reviews were for the most part hostile, some virulently so.[3] Few attempts were made to judge the work by literary standards, and such terms as 'garbage' and 'moral vomit' were applied to it by reviewers who allowed their judgement to be clouded by their feelings about Byron's private life; other notices were, in the manner of the time, coloured by the political prejudices of their authors.[4]

Meanwhile Byron had been going ahead with Canto III. He was undoubtedly put out by the reception of Cantos I and II, but, as his letters to Kinnaird and others testify, he was becoming increasingly confident, in defiance of the 'nonsensical prudery' of his friends, that in *Don Juan* he was doing something extremely worthwhile, and although he had periods of doubt and depression, intensified by domestic and financial worry, the poem continued to grow. In 1819 and 1820 he was a good deal preoccupied with the composition of *The Prophecy of Dante* and the tragedy *Marino Faliero*, with his translation of Pulci, and with a number of other literary projects, but by December 1820 he had completed Canto V of *Don Juan*. After reading the proofs of this canto, he wrote to Murray: 'It will be long before you see anything half so good as poetry or writing;' and a month later: 'I read over the *Juans*, which are excellent.' He was in fact having to goad the timorous and disapproving Murray into publishing the second instalment of his poem, and when Cantos III–V were issued in 1821, the publisher's name did not appear on the title-page.

The reviews of 1821 were not as universally condemnatory as those of 1819; indeed, some of the opinions expressed were flattering. For example, under the *nom de plume* 'John Bull', J. G. Lockhart wrote in a *Letter to the Right Hon. Lord Byron*:

> Stick to Don Juan: it is the only sincere thing you have ever written; and it will live many years after all your humbug Harolds have ceased to be. . . . I consider Don Juan as out of all sight the best of your works; it is by far the most spirited, the most straightforward, the most interesting, and the most poetical; and everybody thinks as I do of it, although they have not the heart to say so.

In spite of such encouragement, Byron now laid the poem aside for eighteen months, partly at the insistence of his mistress, the Countess Guiccioli, who, having read part of it in a French translation, professed herself horrified by it, partly because, with the Countess's brother, he was immersing himself in Italian politics, partly because he was engaged in other literary activities, including the writing of his brilliant satire on Southey, *The Vision of Judgment*, which was published in 1822 in *The Liberal*, the short-lived journal which he and Leigh Hunt founded in that year.

It is difficult to believe that during these months Byron would entirely have neglected a project so near to his heart as *Don Juan*, and it is likely that Canto VI was complete, or nearly so, when in the summer of 1822 the Countess Guiccioli lifted her ban. In June he took up the poem again in earnest, and in the following month, with more than a touch of humour, he wrote to Murray: 'I obtained permission from my Dictatress to continue it,—*provided always* it was to be more guarded and decorous and sentimental in the continuation than in the commencement.' It may be wondered whether the Countess would have found Canto VI, which relates Juan's experiences in a harem, 'more guarded and decorous', or the later cantos more sentimental, than what had come before. Warming to his task, Byron raced through ten further cantos in a sustained and splendid burst of creativity, completing Canto XVI in March 1823. Although this canto brings us to a point of considerable interest in Juan's career, Byron's activities in the cause of Greek independence allowed him no time to proceed further, and the last stanzas leave us in suspense—a suspense which is not relieved by the fifteen stanzas that he wrote for Canto XVII. Cantos VI–XIV were published in 1823, and XV–XVI in the following year. Murray had declined their publication, which was entrusted to Leigh Hunt's brother, John Hunt. The poem was published complete in 1826.

4

THE LATER CANTOS

This volume presents two self-contained episodes in the career of Byron's Don Juan, linked by the narrative of the sea-voyage, the storm, the shipwreck, and Juan's arrival on Lambro's island. However, these episodes cannot, in fairness to Byron and his purposes, be considered without some reference to their place in the poem as a whole, and the following summary of the later cantos is provided in order to fill in a more complete background for the critical comments which follow.

Our selection breaks off with the death of Haidée about three-quarters of the way through Canto IV. The remainder of the canto tells how Juan and a number of other captives of Lambro are shipped to Constantinople to be sold as slaves.

In Canto V we are taken to the slave-market, where Juan and a new acquaintance, an English soldier-adventurer named Johnson, are bought by an old black eunuch and conveyed to the Sultan's palace. Here, despite his protests, Juan is 'femininely all array'd', and with his slimness and his good looks he appears 'in almost all respects a maid'. The reason for this transformation is soon revealed. The Sultana Gulbeyaz, the reigning favourite among the Sultan's fifteen hundred concubines, had seen Juan 'on his way to sale', and, falling in love with him at first sight, had ordered him to be purchased and brought to her. There follows a richly comic interview, in which the Sultana, used to having all her desires satisfied, finds her advances repulsed by Juan. All her conflicting passions are minutely described. The interview (and with it the canto) is brought to an end by the sudden arrival of the Sultan. Among the many digressions are a largely serious meditation on mortality, and satirical reflections on the *longueurs* of travel books, and on other women—Potiphar's wife, Lady Booby, and Phaedra—whose love has been scorned.

At the beginning of Canto VI Juan, still dressed as an odalisque, is compelled by the Sultan's arrival to withdraw into the harem. As the newest 'wife', he is an object of much interest to the others, especially to Lolah, Katinka, and Dudù —three very different ideals of feminine beauty. It grows late, and there is no bed for 'Juanna'; she has to share Dudù's. The silence of the night is broken by a scream from Dudù, which, 'with some confusion', she explains as having been caused by a nightmare, whereupon the girls return to their beds. In the morning Gulbeyaz questions the eunuch Baba, and in a frenzy of jealousy orders Juan and Dudù to be put to death. The canto is a characteristically Byronic blend of high comedy and high beauty, the one provided by the action, the other by descriptions of the odalisques and of the sleeping harem. Once again there are ironic or satirical digressions—on Antony and

Cleopatra, on the Age of Gold, on pins in women's dresses; and once again there are serious reflections on the purpose of life.

Cantos VII and VIII relate the siege and capture of Ismail during the Russian–Turkish war. Escaped from Constantinople, Juan and Johnson arrive on the eve of the final assault, and are welcomed by the Russian commander, Field-Marshal Souvaroff. They fight bravely, and in the course of the battle Juan rescues a little Moslem orphan girl, Leila, who accompanies him on his later travels, and whose religious sentiments and observances prompt in Byron some ironic reflections on the outward forms of different religions. For his distinguished services Juan is chosen to carry Souvaroff's dispatches to Catherine the Great at St. Petersburg. What 'happens' in these cantos is of less importance than Byron's reflections. The true theme of the cantos is the horror of war and the emptiness of military 'Glory'. There are vivid descriptions of acts of heroism and self-sacrifice and humanity, but these, seen against the background of senseless carnage and military and political vanity and chicanery and lust for power, merely emphasise the force of Byron's feelings about the futility of military ambition and the nothingness of military glory.

'Let there be Light!' said God, and there was Light!
'Let there be Blood!' says man, and there's a sea!

Byron is especially deeply shocked by Souvaroff's dispatch:

'Glory to *God* and to the Empress!' (*Powers
Eternal! such names mingled!*) 'Ismail's ours.'

These, he thinks, are 'the most tremendous words, Since "Mené, Mené, Tekel," and "Upharsin".' In these cantos Byron the moralist and lover of man for the first time takes clear precedence over Byron the chronicler.

Cantos IX and X describe Juan's life in St. Petersburg. Catherine the Great falls in love with him, and he is raised to the 'high official station' of favourite. His Spanish relatives write to him, hoping through him to get preferment to important offices in Russia, and he learns that Donna Inez has presented him with a brother, presumably as the

wife of Don Alfonso. However, Juan's life amid the cares
and intrigues of the court, and as the 'favourite' of the Empress,
does not suit him; he falls ill, and barely survives the minis-
trations of the doctors, and for his health's sake Catherine
sends him to England as her envoy on a diplomatic mission.
Juan and Leila travel through Poland, Germany, and Holland,
are fleeced by the Customs at Dover, and make their way
towards London. Among the digressions in these cantos are an
apostrophe to Hypocrisy, and meditations on corruption in
high places, on the 'decaying fame and former worth' of
England, and once again on the theme 'What a strange thing
is man!'

Cantos XI–XVI, the 'English' cantos, may be taken together. Approaching London, Juan soliloquises on the happy
lot of those who live in England:

> 'And here,' he cried, 'is Freedom's chosen station;
>   Here peals the people's voice . . .
> Here laws are all inviolate; none lay
>   Traps for the traveller; every highway's clear;
> Here'—he was interrupted by a knife,
> With—'Damn your eyes! your money or your life!'

'These freeborn sounds' proceed from four footpads, whom
Juan drives off, killing one. In London he cuts a figure in the
worlds of diplomacy and of high society; he is taken up by
Lord Henry and Lady Adeline Amundeville, and joins a house-
party at their country seat, Norman Abbey—an opportunity
for Byron to write a beautiful description of Newstead Abbey.
Juan pleases the men by his prowess in the hunting-field, and
charms the ladies by his address in the drawing-room, especially the amorous and amoral Duchess of Fitz-Fulke. Neglected
by her politician husband, Lady Adeline takes a particular
interest in Juan, and her conflicting emotions towards him are
dissected in some detail. However, she sets about finding a
wife for him, and in this context we meet Aurora Raby, in the
description of whom Byron appears to be setting up an ideal of
beautiful and virtuous English womanhood, untainted by the
sophistication of the society in which she moves, as earlier
Haidée had represented an ideal of natural beauty and innocence, untainted by the artifices of civilisation. One night at

Norman Abbey, Juan's sleep is broken by a ghostly visitant, which troubles his thoughts. The poem ends with a second visitation, when the apparition reveals itself as 'The phantom of her frolic Grace—Fitz-Fulke!'

The narrative thread of these last six cantos is very thin; it is supplied very largely by descriptions of Juan's participation in the activities (or lack of activity) of the leisured and aristocratic men and women of Byron's day—dinner-parties, field-sports, drawing-room chit-chat and scandal, political and amorous intrigue—all recounted with great liveliness, in a spirit now of fun, now of irony, now of withering satire. These cantos are valuable chiefly as the most comprehensive and penetrating satire we possess of English men and manners in a particular era. No side of social or political life is neglected, and the heaviest satire is directed against the types of men and women with whom Byron had been most intimately acquainted in his earlier years in London, especially against the uselessness and selfishness of their lives:

Society is now one polished horde,
Formed of two mighty tribes, the *Bores* and *Bored*.

Idleness and boredom are, in Byron's view, the two greatest dangers in human society, for they can breed nothing but mischief.

It will be apparent from this summary that the early cantos represented in the present selection are far from revealing every side of Byron's genius in its maturity. From a poem which was at first 'meant to be a little quietly facetious upon everything', *Don Juan* develops into a vast panorama of European life, especially English life, in the first decades of the nineteenth century. From the 'naughtiness' of the earlier episodes—punctuated, however, by the reflections upon life of a sober and thinking man—it develops into a poem which, while it continues to be quietly facetious upon almost everything, is nevertheless the work of a serious moralist—in Shelley's words, 'something wholly new and relative to the age, and yet surpassingly beautiful'.

5

THE POEM

'My poem's epic,' says Byron near the end of the first canto, and he goes on to list its epic attributes: 'divided in twelve books'—though indeed it grew to more; its subjects

> . . . love and war, a heavy gale at sea,
>   A list of ships, and captains, and kings reigning;
> New characters; the episodes are three:
>   A panorama view of hell's in training,
> After the style of Virgil and of Homer,
> So that my name of Epic's no misnomer.

In the next stanza he speaks of his 'new mythological machinery, And very handsome supernatural scenery'. All these elements are to be handled 'With strict regard to Aristotle's rules, The *vade mecum* of the true sublime'. Byron's tongue is in his cheek, of course; nevertheless, it will be worthwhile to examine the claims of *Don Juan* to be regarded as an epic, which is generally held to be one of the highest forms of literary composition.

Clearly the poem is not a heroic epic of the Homeric–Virgilian–Miltonic type, nor a didactic epic of the type exemplified in Hesiod's *Works and Days*, Virgil's *Georgics*, or Milton's *Paradise Regained*; it is not a serious epic of any kind—which, however, is not to say that it is not a serious poem of any kind. The way in which Byron relates the Juan–Julia *affaire*, and the tone—comic, ironic, satiric—of the first canto, and indeed of the poem as a whole, are scarcely appropriate to serious epic. Nor does Byron fulfil all the promises that he embodies in his claim. He supplies no mythological machinery, and no supernatural scenery such as he sketches so delightfully in *The Vision of Judgment*, and such as would presumably have been required if he had provided his panoramic view of hell. In speaking of hell, Byron is obviously thinking of the traditional forms of the Don Juan legend, in which the hero is snatched away to hell. That he might conceivably have adopted this feature of the legend, had his poem turned out differently, is suggested by an ironic comment in a letter which he wrote to John Murray in 1821: 'I had not quite fixed whether to make him end in Hell or in an unhappy marriage, not knowing which would be the severest.' However, the development of *Don Juan*, and its form, were determined in the course of the years by the poet's personal experiences, his reading, and his changing interests and preoccupations, and perhaps above all by his increasingly serious concern with the vacuity of most people's lives, with the futility of ambitious pretensions, with man's inhumanity to man, and with the purpose of life. As Juan's education in the ways of the world proceeds, it becomes less and less likely that he will end his days in the arms of devils who have been sent to carry him to hell. Whether Byron intended, by a final twist of irony at the end of the poem, to consign him to the arms of an uncongenial wife cannot be known; from the tenor of the last cantos this seems to me just as unlikely as the previous alternative.

When Byron uses epic devices 'after the style of Virgil and of Homer', he does so for comic purposes. He provides several epic catalogues—of potential candidates for the role of hero; of Russians immortalised by their valour in the Siege of Ismail, such as 'Tschitsshakoff, and Roguenoff, and Chokenoff, And others of twelve consonants apiece'; of guests at Lady Adeline's house-party; of suitable brides for Juan. Always he turns such catalogues to comic or satiric effect, or gives them a comic or satiric setting. He uses epic invocations at appropriate points —'Hail, Muse! et caetera!' or 'Oh, thou, Eternal Homer' when he is to paint a siege. He uses a great many epic apostrophes— 'Oh, Love!' or 'Oh, blood and thunder! and oh, blood and wounds!' or 'Oh for a *forty-parson power* to chant Thy praise, Hypocrisy!' Here again, even where such invocations and apostrophes are, or appear to be, used in a serious context, it will almost invariably be found, either that they are being used ironically, or that the reflections to which they lead are given an ironic turn. The poem treats themes that are traditionally associated with the epic—war, journeys undertaken by or imposed on the hero, tempest and shipwreck, love—and Byron's handling of these themes is productive of some of his most beautiful and impressive poetry. However, he will never allow himself to remain for long on the heroic plane, or any high plane. His accounts of deeds of valour and self-sacrifice in battle are used to point his satire of what passes by the name of glory; his sombrely magnificent narrative of the shipwreck and the drifting in the long-boat contains many touches of comedy and deliberate bathos; and even the lovely descriptions of the idyllic love of Juan and Haidée are punctuated by ironic reflections.

On first impressions, then, it would seem a characteristically Byronic leg-pull to label his poem an epic, and so in a sense it is, in the context in which he does so. Nevertheless, in certain fundamental senses of the term, the 'name of Epic's no misnomer'. An epic poem is, among other things, a narrative poem on the grand scale; we expect of it a wide sweep, a vast range of human experience, of human activity and feeling. No one would dispute that *Don Juan* has these attributes. We expect of the epic that it should deal with matters of universal human concern. Now in the early cantos Byron appears to be chiefly interested in telling stories, and is not averse from shocking his readers almost, it seems at times, for the sake of shocking; but even in these cantos he shows, for the most part in his asides and digressions, a continual awareness of what must be of serious concern to all men—the character of love, the motives of human actions and the value of human aspirations, the difference between civilisation and nature, between false seeming and truth, between appearance and reality. As the poem proceeds, and the digressions to an ever-increasing degree take precedence over the narration, his study of the hearts and minds of men and his questioning of the purposes for which we are given life become increasingly profound and an increasingly important element of his poem. It may be objected that he scarcely treats these subjects with the seriousness which they demand, and which we expect of the epic poet. Certainly *Don Juan* contains much triviality and much fooling—it has already been conceded that it is not a serious epic; but the reader soon learns—he must learn—to read between the lines, to see beneath the flippancy and the cynicism the serious purport of what the poet is saying. Like many sensitive people, Byron wears a mask to hide his feelings, but he cannot for long hide his intense seriousness when he is speaking of such intensely serious things as, for example, liberty, or war, or any form of pretentiousness or humbug.

Taking up the question from a different angle—the epic poets of the Renaissance aimed at combining profit with delight, believing, as Horace had taught them in the *Ars Poetica*, that

> omne tulit punctum qui miscuit utile dulci,
> lectorem delectando pariterque monendo.
>
> *(A.P.* 343-44)

Spenser, for example, tells us that 'the generall end' of *The Faerie Queene* 'is to fashion a gentleman or noble person in vertuous and gentle discipline'. It is perhaps unlikely that in the early stages of the composition Byron had any such end as this in view, and questionable whether even in the later stages he was thinking clearly along these lines. Nevertheless, it is impossible not to feel that, as the poem grew, he felt, perhaps only subconsciously, an ever-increasing urge to mingle profit with the delight which probably remained his chief conscious purpose. Those who read the whole poem may well see as one element of the profit something akin to the fashioning of a gentleman or noble person in virtuous and gentle discipline. I am not suggesting that Byron's conception of such a discipline was the same as Spenser's; among other reasons why this should not be so, the ages in which the two poets lived were very different. But as Byron found himself able to allow more and more of himself, of his mind and heart and experience of life, to flow into the poem, we become ever more conscious that we are spectators of what I earlier called Juan's education in the ways of the world. He passes through many kinds of experience, and gets to know men and women of every type; he learns something of value from each of his experiences— tolerance, tact, compassion, how to conduct himself in affairs of all kinds; though he is sometimes made to look foolish, he does nothing that could seriously be held to his discredit, and much that is creditable and honourable; at the end of the poem he is astonishingly thoughtful and mature for a young man of eighteen or twenty-one—a discrepancy as to his age creeps in near the end. He is well on the way to becoming such a man as Byron could perhaps have wished himself to be.

If in the light of this discussion it can be accepted that *Don Juan* possesses many of the essential properties of the epic, it remains to be determined what kind of epic. In an earlier section reference has been made to Byron's debt to the 'jocose' epics of the Italian poets for the manner of *Beppo* and

Don Juan. But a very wide range of reading of other kinds also lies behind *Don Juan*, as indeed is testified by the innumerable quotations and literary allusions embodied in the poem.[5] Among Byron's favourite English authors were Fielding and Smollett, especially Fielding, whom he describes in one of his anti-Bowles letters as 'the man of education, the gentleman, and the scholar, sporting with his subject—its master, not its slave'. Possibly Byron saw something of himself in this description—not unjustly, if it were so. However that may be, among the most influential 'models' of *Don Juan* is the picaresque novel, and of picaresque novels perhaps especially those of Fielding—discursive, rambling, yet unified by the central figure of the hero and by a clearly revealed and consistent philosophy of life and moral purpose, often ironic in tone, punctuated by the reflections of the author. There is much, too, that is reminiscent of Tom Jones in the adventures, the make-up, and the development of Don Juan. In the Preface to *Joseph Andrews* Fielding describes his novels as comic epic poems in prose. *Don Juan* may also be described as a comic epic poem. However, it is more than merely comic; more frequently and more overtly than Fielding's novels, it is satirical. If we are to find a label which, while modifying Byron's claim for the work, does not conflict with it, we can do no better than describe *Don Juan* as the great epic satire of our literature.

This is no place to embark on a general study of Byron's books as formative influences in the writing of *Don Juan*, although, as the notes in this volume abundantly illustrate, he was a voracious and retentive reader. However, mention should be made of one further class of books which undoubtedly helped to shape the poem, and this is the class which embraces such works as Rabelais' *Gargantua and Pantagruel*, Butler's *Hudibras*, and Sterne's *Tristram Shandy*. The three works make strange bedfellows, indeed, but the first two show some affinity in their combination of burlesque adventure-narrative with fantasy and satire on contemporary events and institutions and with the exposition of serious and deeply-felt convictions, and Rabelais and Sterne are both masters of the purposive digression, communicating some of their most memorable reflections and gaining some of their highest artistic effects by means of digression, or digression arising out of digression. The relationship between these works and *Don Juan* need not be developed here. I have already spoken of its fundamental seriousness; the burlesque, the fantasy, and the satire are everywhere apparent; and a few minutes' reading, especially in the later cantos, will suffice to show how much it depends on digression both for its artistic effects and for the communication of its deeper meaning.

Nor, in the light of what has already been said, need much time be spent on another of Byron's claims. Both within the poem and in his conversation and letters, he always insisted that it was a moral work: 'I maintain that it is the most moral of poems; but if people won't discover the moral, that is their fault, not mine.' The first readers of the early cantos for the most part saw, were often determined to see, only their 'naughtiness', and, according to the nature of their prejudices against Byron, magnified it into the worst forms of immorality. However, it is possible to see an essentially moral mind at work even in Canto I. Beneath the ironic and irreverent portrait of Donna Inez and the satire on Lady Byron that it embodies, there lies scorn for the follies of the educational system that she imposed on Juan, and of the false pretenders to learning that she represents, and by implication respect for what is negated by these follies. The comedy of the Juan–Julia *fabliau* is interrupted by asides and digressions which manifest a similar scorn for cant and hypocrisy and every kind of false seeming. And the Juan–Haidée idyll may be interpreted, again largely from the incidental comment, as an exposure of the false artifices of modern civilisation. The morality becomes clearer and more insistent as the poem progresses. It may be felt that it is presented in a predominantly negative way, and that a more convinced moralist than Byron would have found more positive ways of revealing his love for what is good and true. However, Byron's method is that of many great moralists, such as Lucian, or Sir Thomas More, or Swift. By showing men what they ought not to be and ought not to do, these writers force them to ponder upon what they ought to be and ought to do. Their moral attitude is implicit rather than explicit.

Had Byron had the immoral designs that were attributed to him, he would scarcely have taken the pains he did to make his hero so very different from previous Don Juans. The Don

Juan of the legend is a reckless and cynical profligate. Byron's Juan, unnaturally sheltered from knowledge of illicit love, even of the amours of classical gods and goddesses, is exceptionally naïve and innocent when he is taken in hand by the Donna Julia. His love for Julia is the first love of a callow boy, sweet, but bewildered and diffident; it is she who makes the advances, and Juan alone remains untainted by the cant and hypocrisy of the social background against which the episode is set. His love for Haidée is passionate, but absolutely natural and absolutely pure. He rejects the love of the Sultana Gulbeyaz. Whatever happens during the night in the harem when he has to share a bed with Dudù, it can scarcely be taken as evidence that he is a profligate. His love for the orphan Leila is all that is generous and unselfish. His relations with Catherine the Great appear to be those of a reluctant lover; and in the final episode the Duchess of Fitz-Fulke is the pursuer, and there is nothing to suggest that he will allow himself to be caught by her, or even that his vanity is touched by her flattering attentions, as perhaps it was by those of Catherine the Great. Too much has been made of the 'love-interest' of *Don Juan*, and too often it has been assumed, without support from the poem, that Juan's morals as a lover deteriorate, that he becomes increasingly unscrupulous. The truth is that, after the early cantos, his experience of love forms a comparatively small part of the experience of life by which his character is being formed; and in none of his dealings with women does he do anything that entitles us to regard him as a libertine. The Don Juan legend required that its hero should be pictured as a lover, but Byron's treatment of love in his *Don Juan* does no serious damage to his claim that it is a moral poem—rather the reverse when the attitudes he reveals towards ill-governed or false or illicit love are taken into account.

Among those who early recognised the essential morality of *Don Juan* was Shelley, who, having read the first five cantos, wrote to Byron:

Nothing has ever been written like it in English, nor, if I may venture to prophesy, will there be. . . . You unveil and present in its true deformity what is worst in human nature, and this is what the witlings of the age murmur at, conscious of their want of power to endure the scrutiny of such light. . . . You are building up a drama, such as England has not yet seen, and the task is sufficiently noble and worthy of you.

We may turn now to the style and presentation of *Don Juan*. 'Style' is perhaps a misleading word, for the poem is a compound of many styles, or tones. Indeed, what above all gives it its special character is its versatility and unpredictability of tone, its sudden but carefully contrived transitions from the serious to the trivial, from the pathetic to the ironic, from the sublime to the grotesque. It may be suggested that the comparative neglect that Byron suffered in England in the last decades of the nineteenth and the early decades of the twentieth centuries was at least partly caused by the fondness of our grandparents for volumes of 'elegant extracts' and 'great thoughts'. The mature Byron does not stand up well to being read in extracts. His passages of supreme beauty—Juan and Haidée walking hand in hand along the beach; of high pathos—the death of Haidée; of ironic reflection—'that love and marriage rarely can combine'; of withering invective—Castlereagh, the 'cold-blooded, smooth-faced, placid miscreant'; of light comedy—Juan fleeing from Julia's chamber, and, like Joseph, leaving his only garment behind; of grim comedy—the death of Juan's tutor; of sombre grandeur—the shipwreck: these and countless other memorable passages gain their full effect only when they are seen jostling one another in a large context. It is the juxtaposition of different styles and tones and themes, the great variety of characters and incidents, the digressions relevant and irrelevant, that make up what has been called 'Don Juanism'. The poem is a great satire not only as we understand satire, but also in the original Roman sense of the term, that is, a medley of different subjects and styles and moods, all contributing to a total effect.

The prevailing tone is ironically humorous. Byron can drop this tone at will, according to his purpose for the moment, but it is always there in the background, to be picked up again at will. The prevailing style is conversational. It is essentially the style of a witty and intelligent and cultivated man talking to his friends after dinner, at his ease and relaxed, retailing now anecdotes, now reflections grave or gay, now caustic comments on the affairs and personalities of the day. It is, indeed,

c

remarkably like the actual conversation of Byron, if we may judge from contemporary reports. In her *Recollections of Lord Byron* the Countess Guiccioli quotes Colonel Stanhope as saying:

> As a companion . . . no one could be more amusing than Lord Byron; he had neither pedantry nor affectation about him, but was natural and playful as a boy. His conversation resembled a stream; sometimes smooth, sometimes rapid, and sometimes rushing down in cataracts. It was a mixture of philosophy and slang, of everything,—like his 'Don Juan'.

Byron's conversation seems to have been great fun; *Don Juan* is also great fun.

Byron has at his command all the stylistic tricks of the comic poet—puns, *double entendre*, incongruous quotation and allusion, anticlimax, deliberate bathos. All these devices are used too frequently to require illustration here. It was in a happy hour that he hit upon the *ottava rima* stanza for his vehicle, and discovered its potentialities for his purposes in *Beppo*, *Don Juan*, and *The Vision of Judgment*. Although he can strike out happy epigrams, his genius is, on the whole, expansive, and the eight-line stanza allows him plenty of room for the development of a picture or a reflection. The alternate rhyme on two sounds in the first six lines is both a challenge and an opportunity, and while he is very rarely at a loss for the fitting rhyme when he is aiming at a grave or a beautiful effect, he is quick to see the value of a ridiculous rhyme when he is aiming at a comic or a satirical effect. He makes excellent use of the final couplet of the stanza—to clinch a reflection with an epigram, or to achieve a climax, an anticlimax, or a surprise ending:

> He learn'd the arts of riding, fencing, gunnery,
> And how to scale a fortress—or a nunnery.

He outdoes Butler himself in his handling of the 'hudibrastic' rhyme, as in the famous

> But—Oh! ye lords of ladies intellectual,
> Inform us truly, have they not hen-peck'd you all?

However, the individual tricks of style must not, any more than the other elements of the poem, be divorced from their context; they are part of a total effect, and, as I have been at pains to point out, in *Don Juan*, as indeed in any great work of art, the total effect is all-important. The style, we are told, is the man. In speaking of so heterogeneous a work as *Don Juan*, we may perhaps put it in another way, and say that the poem is the man. For what places *Don Juan* among the great poems of our literature is that it is, in a fuller sense than almost any other poem of comparable scope, the complete self-expression of a rich and creative mind and of a rich and fascinating personality.

NOTES

1. *The Metamorphoses of Don Juan*, by Leo Weinstein. Stanford U.P. and O.U.P., 1959.

2. All the dramatic versions named in this paragraph are printed in whole or in part, where necessary in English translations, in *The Theatre of Don Juan: A Collection of Plays and Views*, ed. by Oscar Mandel. Nebraska U.P., 1963.

3. For a full account of the reception of *Don Juan* see *The Flowering of Byron's Genius: Studies in Byron's Don Juan*, by Paul G. Trueblood. Stanford U.P., 1945.

4. See 'The Publishing of Byron's *Don Juan*', by H. J. Luke, in *Publications of the Modern Language Association of America (PMLA)*, June 1965.

5. For Byron's reading see, e.g., *Byron's 'Don Juan': A Critical Study*, by Elizabeth French Boyd. Routledge and Kegan Paul, 1958, chaps. 6, 7, 8.

DON JUAN

DEDICATION

I

Bob Southey! You're a poet—Poet-laureate,
  And representative of all the race,
Although 'tis true that you turn'd out a Tory at
  Last,—yours has lately been a common case,—
And now, my Epic Renegade! what are ye at?
  With all the Lakers, in and out of place?
A nest of tuneful persons, to my eye
Like 'four and twenty Blackbirds in a pye;

II

'Which pye being open'd they began to sing'
  (This old song and new simile holds good),
'A dainty dish to set before the King',
  Or Regent, who admires such kind of food;—
And Coleridge, too, has lately taken wing,
  But like a hawk encumber'd with his hood,—
Explaining metaphysics to the nation—
I wish he would explain his Explanation.

III

You, Bob! are rather insolent, you know,
  At being disappointed in your wish
To supersede all warblers here below,
  And be the only Blackbird in the dish;
And then you overstrain yourself, or so,
  And tumble downward like the flying fish
Gasping on deck, because you soar too high, Bob,
And fall, for lack of moisture quite a-dry, Bob!

IV

And Wordsworth, in a rather long 'Excursion'
    (I think the quarto holds five hundred pages),
Has given a sample from the vasty version
    Of his new system to perplex the sages;
'Tis poetry—at least by his assertion,
    And may appear so when the dog-star rages—
And he who understands it would be able
To add a story to the Tower of Babel.

V

You—Gentlemen! by dint of long seclusion
    From better company, have kept your own
At Keswick, and, through still continued fusion
    Of one another's minds, at last have grown
To deem as a most logical conclusion,
    That Poesy has wreaths for you alone:
There is a narrowness in such a notion,
Which makes me wish you'd change your lakes for ocean

VI

I would not imitate the petty thought,
    Nor coin my self-love to so base a vice,
For all the glory your conversion brought,
    Since gold alone should not have been its price.
You have your salary; was't for that you wrought?
    And Wordsworth has his place in the Excise.
You're shabby fellows—true—but poets still,
And duly seated on the immortal hill.

VII

Your bays may hide the baldness of your brows—
    Perhaps some virtuous blushes;—let them go—
To you I envy neither fruit nor boughs—
    And for the fame you would engross below,

The field is universal, and allows
   Scope to all such as feel the inherent glow:
Scott, Rogers, Campbell, Moore, and Crabbe, will try
'Gainst you the question with posterity.

VIII

For me, who, wandering with pedestrian Muses,
   Contend not with you on the winged steed,
I wish your fate may yield ye, when she chooses,
   The fame you envy, and the skill you need;
And recollect a poet nothing loses
   In giving to his brethren their full meed
Of merit, and complaint of present days
Is not the certain path to future praise.

IX

He that reserves his laurels for posterity
   (Who does not often claim the bright reversion)
Has generally no great crop to spare it, he
   Being only injured by his own assertion;
And although here and there some glorious rarity
   Arise like Titan from the sea's immersion,
The major part of such appellants go
To—God knows where—for no one else can know.

X

If, fallen in evil days on evil tongues,
   Milton appealed to the Avenger, Time,
If Time, the Avenger, execrates his wrongs,
   And makes the word 'Miltonic' means '*sublime*',
He deign'd not to belie his soul in songs,
   Nor turn his very talent to a crime;
He did not loathe the Sire to laud the Son,
But closed the tyrant-hater he begun.

XI

Think'st thou, could he—the blind Old Man—arise
　　Like Samuel from the grave, to freeze once more
The blood of monarchs with his prophecies,
　　Or be alive again—again all hoar
With time and trials, and those helpless eyes,
　　And heartless daughters—worn—and pale—and poor;
Would *he* adore a sultan? *he* obey
The intellectual eunuch Castlereagh?

XII

Cold-blooded, smooth-faced, placid miscreant!
　　Dabbling its sleek young hands in Erin's gore,
And thus for wider carnage taught to pant,
　　Transferr'd to gorge upon a sister shore,
The vulgarest tool that Tyranny could want,
　　With just enough of talent, and no more,
To lengthen fetters by another fix'd,
And offer poison long already mix'd.

XIII

An orator of such set trash of phrase
　　Ineffably—legitimately vile,
That even its grossest flatterers dare not praise,
　　Nor foes—all nations—condescend to smile;
Not even a sprightly blunder's spark can blaze
　　From that Ixion grindstone's ceaseless toil,
That turns and turns to give the world a notion
Of endless torments and perpetual motion.

XIV

A bungler even in its disgusting trade,
　　And botching, patching, leaving still behind
Something of which its masters are afraid,
　　States to be curb'd, and thoughts to be confined,

Conspiracy or Congress to be made—
   Cobbling at manacles for all mankind—
A tinkering slave-maker, who mends old chains,
With God and man's abhorrence for its gains.

XV

If we may judge of matter by the mind,
   Emasculated to the marrow *It*
Hath but two objects, how to serve, and bind,
   Deeming the chain it wears even men may fit,
Eutropius of its many masters,—blind
   To worth as freedom, wisdom as to wit,
Fearless—because *no* feeling dwells in ice,
Its very courage stagnates to a vice.

XVI

Where shall I turn me not to *view* its bonds,
   For I will never *feel* them;—Italy!
Thy late reviving Roman soul desponds
   Beneath the lie this State-thing breathed o'er thee—
Thy clanking chain, and Erin's yet green wounds,
   Have voices—tongues to cry aloud for me.
Europe has slaves—allies—kings—armies still,
And Southey lives to sing them very ill.

XVII

Meantime—Sir Laureate—I proceed to dedicate,
   In honest simple verse, this song to you.
And, if in flattering strains I do not predicate,
   'Tis that I still retain my 'buff and blue';
My politics as yet are all to educate;
   Apostasy's so fashionable, too,
To keep *one* creed's a task grown quite Herculean;
Is it not so, my Tory, Ultra-Julian?

CANTO I

I

I want a hero: an uncommon want,
  When every year and month sends forth a new one,
Till, after cloying the gazettes with cant,
  The age discovers he is not the true one:
Of such as these I should not care to vaunt,
  I'll therefore take our ancient friend Don Juan—
We all have seen him, in the Pantomime
Sent to the devil, somewhat ere his time.

II

Vernon, the butcher Cumberland, Wolfe, Hawke,
  Prince Ferdinand, Granby, Burgoyne, Keppel, Howe,
Evil and good, have had their tithe of talk,
  And fill'd their sign-posts then, like Wellesley now;
Each in their turn like Banquo's monarchs stalk,
  Followers of fame, 'nine farrow' of that sow:
France, too, had Buonaparté and Demourier
Recorded in the Moniteur and Courier.

III

Barnave, Brissot, Condorcet, Mirabeau,
  Pétion, Clootz, Danton, Marat, La Fayette,
Were French, and famous people, as we know;
  And there were others, scarce forgotten yet,
Joubert, Houche, Marceau, Lannes, Dessaix, Moreau,
  With many of the military set,
Exceedingly remarkable at times,
But not at all adapted to my rhymes.

IV

Nelson was once Britannia's god of war,
    And still should be so, but the tide is turn'd;
There's no more to be said of Trafalgar,
    'Tis with our hero quietly inurn'd;
Because the army's grown more popular,
    At which the naval people are concern'd,
Besides, the prince is all for the land-service,
Forgetting Duncan, Nelson, Howe, and Jervis.

V

Brave men were living before Agamemnon
    And since, exceeding valorous and sage,
A good deal like him too, though quite the same none;
    But then they shone not on the poet's page,
And so have been forgotten;—I condemn none,
    But can't find any in the present age
Fit for my poem (that is, for my new one);
So, as I said, I'll take my friend Don Juan.

VI

Most epic poets plunge 'in medias res',
    (Horace makes this the heroic turnpike road)
And then your hero tells, whene'er you please,
    What went before—by way of episode,
While seated after dinner at his ease,
    Beside his mistress in some soft abode,
Palace, or garden, paradise, or cavern,
Which serves the happy couple for a tavern.

VII

That is the usual method, but not mine—
    My way is to begin with the beginning;
The regularity of my design
    Forbids all wandering as the worst of sinning,

And therefore I shall open with a line
   (Although it cost me half an hour in spinning)
Narrating somewhat of Don Juan's father,
And also of his mother, if you'd rather.

VIII

In Seville was he born, a pleasant city,
   Famous for oranges and women—he
Who has not seen it will be much to pity,
   So says the proverb—and I quite agree;
Of all the Spanish towns is none more pretty,
   Cadiz, perhaps—but that you soon may see:—
Don Juan's parents lived beside the river,
A noble stream, and call'd the Guadalquivir.

IX

His father's name was Jóse—*Don*, of course,
   A true Hidalgo, free from every stain
Of Moor or Hebrew blood, he traced his source
   Through the most Gothic gentlemen of Spain;
A better cavalier ne'er mounted horse,
   Or, being mounted, e'er got down again,
Than Jóse, who begot our hero, who
Begot—but that's to come——Well, to renew:

X

His mother was a learned lady, famed
   For every branch of every science known—
In every Christian language ever named,
   With virtues equall'd by her wit alone,
She made the cleverest people quite ashamed,
   And even the good with inward envy groan,
Finding themselves so very much exceeded
In their own way by all the things that she did.

XI

Her memory was a mine: she knew by heart
    All Calderon and greater part of Lopé,
So that if any actor miss'd his part
    She could have served him for the prompter's copy;
For her Feinagle's were an useless art,
    And he himself obliged to shut up shop—he
Could never make a memory so fine as
That which adorn'd the brain of Donna Inez.

XII

Her favourite science was the mathematical,
    Her noblest virtue was her magnanimity,
Her wit (she sometimes tried at wit) was Attic all,
    Her serious sayings darken'd to sublimity;
In short, in all things she was fairly what I call
    A prodigy—her morning dress was dimity,
Her evening silk, or, in the summer, muslin,
And other stuffs, with which I won't stay puzzling.

XIII

She knew the Latin—that is, 'the Lord's prayer',
    And Greek—the alphabet—I'm nearly sure;
She read some French romances here and there,
    Although her mode of speaking was not pure;
For native Spanish she had no great care,
    At least her conversation was obscure;
Her thoughts were theorems, her words a problem,
And if she deem'd that mystery would ennoble 'em.

XIV

She liked the English and the Hebrew tongue,
    And said there was analogy between 'em;
She proved it somehow out of sacred song,
    But I must leave the proofs to those who've seen 'em,

But this I heard her say, and can't be wrong,
　　And all may think which way their judgments lean 'em,
' 'Tis strange—the Hebrew noun which means "I am,"
The English always use to govern d—n.'

XV

Some women use their tongues—she *look'd* a lecture,
　　Each eye a sermon, and her brow a homily,
An all-in-all sufficient self-director,
　　Like the lamented late Sir Samuel Romilly,
The Law's expounder, and the State's corrector,
　　Whose suicide was almost an anomaly—
One sad example more, that 'All is vanity',—
(The jury brought their verdict in 'Insanity').

XVI

In short, she was a walking calculation,
　　Miss Edgeworth's novels stepping from their covers,
Or Mrs. Trimmer's books on education,
　　Or 'Cœlebs' Wife' set out in quest of lovers,
Morality's prim personification,
　　In which not Envy's self a flaw discovers;
To others' share let 'female errors fall',
For she had not even one—the worst of all.

XVII

Oh! she was perfect past all parallel—
　　Of any modern female saint's comparison;
So far above the cunning powers of hell,
　　Her guardian angel had given up his garrison;
Even her minutest motions went as well
　　As those of the best time-piece made by Harrison:
In virtues nothing earthly could surpass her,
Save thine 'incomparable oil', Macassar!

XVIII

Perfect she was, but as perfection is
  Insipid in this naughty world of ours,
Where our first parents never learn'd to kiss
  Till they were exiled from their earlier bowers,
Where all was peace, and innocence, and bliss
  (I wonder how they got through the twelve hours),
Don José, like a lineal son of Eve,
Went plucking various fruit without her leave.

XIX

He was a mortal of the careless kind,
  With no great love for learning, or the learn'd,
Who chose to go where'er he had a mind,
  And never dream'd his lady was concern'd:
The world, as usual, wickedly inclined
  To see a kingdom or a house o'erturn'd,
Whisper'd he had a mistress, some said *two*,
But for domestic quarrels *one* will do.

XX

Now Donna Inez had, with all her merit,
  A great opinion of her own good qualities;
Neglect, indeed, requires a saint to bear it,
  And such, indeed, she was in her moralities;
But then she had a devil of a spirit,
  And sometimes mix'd up fancies with realities,
And let few opportunities escape
Of getting her liege lord into a scrape.

XXI

This was an easy matter with a man
  Oft in the wrong, and never on his guard;
And even the wisest, do the best they can,
  Have moments, hours, and days, so unprepared,

That you might 'brain them with their lady's fan';
    And sometimes ladies hit exceeding hard,
And fans turn into falchions in fair hands,
And why and wherefore no one understands.

XXII

'Tis pity learned virgins ever wed
    With persons of no sort of education,
Or gentlemen, who, though well-born and bred,
    Grow tired of scientific conversation:
I don't choose to say much upon this head,
    I'm a plain man, and in a single station,
But—oh! ye lords of ladies intellectual,
Inform us truly, have they not hen-peck'd you all?

XXIII

Don Jóse and his lady quarrell'd—*why*,
    Not any of the many could divine,
Though several thousand people chose to try,
    'Twas surely no concern of theirs nor mine;
I loathe that low vice—curiosity;
    But if there's anything in which I shine,
'Tis in arranging all my friends' affairs,
Not having, of my own, domestic cares.

XXIV

And so I interfered, and with the best
    Intentions, but their treatment was not kind;
I think the foolish people were possess'd,
    For neither of them could I ever find,
Although their porter afterwards confess'd—
    But that's no matter, and the worst's behind,
For little Juan o'er me threw, down stairs,
A pail of housemaid's water unawares.

XXV

A little curly-headed, good-for-nothing,
  And mischief-making monkey from his birth;
His parents ne'er agreed except in doting
  Upon the most unquiet imp on earth;
Instead of quarrelling, had they been but both in
  Their senses, they'd have sent young master forth
To school, or had him soundly whipp'd at home,
To teach him manners for the time to come.

XXVI

Don Jóse and the Donna Inez led
  For some time an unhappy sort of life,
Wishing each other, not divorced, but dead;
  They lived respectably as man and wife,
Their conduct was exceedingly well-bred,
  And gave no outward signs of inward strife,
Until at length the smother'd fire broke out,
And put the business past all kind of doubt.

XXVII

For Inez call'd some druggist and physicians,
  And tried to prove her loving lord was *mad*,
But as he had some lucid intermissions,
  She next decided he was only *bad*;
Yet when they ask'd her for her depositions,
  No sort of explanation could be had,
Save that her duty both to man and God
Required this conduct—which seem'd very odd. . . .

*   *   *

XXXII

Their friends had tried at reconciliation,
  Then their relations, who made matters worse,
('Twere hard to tell upon a like occasion
  To whom it may be best to have recourse—
D

I can't say much for friend or yet relation):
   The lawyers did their utmost for divorce,
But scarce a fee was paid on either side
Before, unluckily, Don Jóse died.

XXXIII

He died; and most unluckily, because,
   According to all hints I could collect
From counsel learned in those kinds of laws
   (Although their talk's obscure and circumspect),
His death contrived to spoil a charming cause;
   A thousand pities also with respect
To public feeling, which on this occasion
Was manifested in a great sensation.

XXXIV

But ah! he died; and buried with him lay
   The public feeling and the lawyers' fees:
His house was sold, his servants sent away,
   A Jew took one of his two mistresses,
A priest the other—at least so they say:
   I ask'd the doctors after his disease—
He died of the slow fever called the tertian,
And left his widow to her own aversion.

XXXV

Yet Jóse was an honourable man,
   That I must say, who knew him very well;
Therefore his frailties I'll no further scan,
   Indeed there were not many more to tell;
And if his passions now and then outran
   Discretion, and were not so peaceable
As Numa's (who was also named Pompilius),
He had been ill brought up, and was born bilious.

XXXVI

Whate'er might be his worthlessness or worth,
    Poor fellow! he had many things to wound him,
Let's own, since it can do no good on earth,
    It was a trying moment that which found him
Standing alone beside his desolate hearth,
    Where all his household gods lay shiver'd round him;
No choice was left his feelings or his pride,
Save death or Doctors' Commons—so he died.

XXXVII

Dying intestate, Juan was sole heir
    To a chancery suit, and messuages, and lands,
Which, with a long minority and care,
    Promised to turn out well in proper hands:
Inez became sole guardian, which was fair,
    And answer'd but to nature's just demands;
An only son left with an only mother
Is brought up much more wisely than another.

XXXVIII

Sagest of women, even of widows, she
    Resolved that Juan should be quite a paragon,
And worthy of the noblest pedigree:
    (His sire was of Castile, his dam from Arragon).
Then for accomplishments of chivalry,
    In case our lord the king should go to war again,
He learn'd the arts of riding, fencing, gunnery,
And how to scale a fortress—or a nunnery.

XXXIX

But that which Donna Inez most desired,
    And saw into herself each day before all
The learned tutors whom for him she hired,
    Was, that his breeding should be strictly moral;

Much into all his studies she inquired,
    And so they were submitted first to her, all,
Arts, sciences, no branch was made a mystery
To Juan's eyes, excepting natural history.

XL

The languages, especially the dead,
    The sciences, and most of all the abstruse,
The arts, at least all such as could be said
    To be the most remote from common use,
In all these he was much and deeply read;
    But not a page of anything that's loose,
Or hints continuation of the species,
Was ever suffer'd, lest he should grow vicious.

XLI

His classic studies made a little puzzle,
    Because of filthy loves of gods and goddesses,
Who in the earlier ages raised a bustle,
    But never put on pantaloons or boddices;
His reverend tutors had at times a tussle,
    And for their Æneids, Iliads, and Odysseys,
Were forced to make an odd sort of apology,
For Donna Inez dreaded the mythology.

XLII

Ovid's a rake, as half his verses show him,
    Anacreon's morals are a still worse sample,
Catullus scarcely has a decent poem,
    I don't think Sappho's Ode a good example,
Although Longinus tells us there is no hymn
    Where the sublime soars forth on wings more ample;
But Virgil's songs are pure, except that horrid one
Beginning with *Formosum Pastor Corydon.*

XLIII

Lucretius' irreligion is too strong
　　For early stomachs, to prove wholesome food;
I can't help thinking Juvenal was wrong,
　　Although no doubt his real intent was good,
For speaking out so plainly in his song,
　　So much indeed as to be downright rude;
And then what proper person can be partial
To all those nauseous epigrams of Martial?

XLIV

Juan was taught from out the best edition,
　　Expurgated by learned men, who place,
Judiciously, from out the schoolboy's vision,
　　The grosser parts; but, fearful to deface
Too much their modest bard by this omission,
　　And pitying sore this mutilated case,
They only add them all in an appendix,
Which saves, in fact, the trouble of an index. . . .

*　　*　　*

XLVII

Sermons he read, and lectures he endured,
　　And homilies, and lives of all the saints;
To Jerome and to Chrysostom inured,
　　He did not take such studies for restraints;
But how faith is acquired, and then insured,
　　So well not one of the aforesaid paints
As Saint Augustine in his fine Confessions,
Which make the reader envy his transgressions.

XLVIII

This, too, was a seal'd book to little Juan—
　　I can't but say that his mamma was right,
If such an education was the true one.
　　She scarcely trusted him from out her sight;

Her maids were old, and if she took a new one,
　　You might be sure she was a perfect fright,
She did this during even her husband's life—
I recommend as much to every wife.

XLIX

Young Juan wax'd in godliness and grace;
　　At six a charming child, and at eleven
With all the promise of as fine a face
　　As e'er to man's maturer growth was given:
He studied steadily, and grew apace,
　　And seem'd, at least, in the right road to heaven,
For half his days were pass'd at church, the other
Between his tutors, confessor, and mother.

L

At six, I said, he was a charming child,
　　At twelve he was a fine, but quiet boy;
Although in infancy a little wild,
　　They tamed him down amongst them; to destroy
His natural spirit not in vain they toil'd,
　　At least it seem'd so; and his mother's joy
Was to declare how sage, and still, and steady,
Her young philosopher was grown already.

LI

I had my doubts, perhaps I have them still,
　　But what I say is neither here nor there:
I knew his father well, and have some skill
　　In character—but it would not be fair
From sire to son to augur good or ill:
　　He and his wife were an ill-sorted pair—
But scandal's my aversion—I protest
Against all evil speaking, even in jest.

LII

For my part I say nothing—nothing—but
   This I will say—my reasons are my own—
That if I had an only son to put
   To school (as God be praised that I have none),
'Tis not with Donna Inez I would shut
   Him up to learn his catechism alone,
No—no—I'd send him out betimes to college,
For there it was I pick'd up my own knowledge.

LIII

For there one learns—'tis not for me to boast,
   Though I acquired—but I pass over *that*,
As well as all the Greek I since have lost:
   I say that there's the place—but '*Verbum sat*',
I think I pick'd up too, as well as most,
   Knowledge of matters—but no matter *what*—
I never married—but, I think, I know
That sons should not be educated so.

LIV

Young Juan now was sixteen years of age,
   Tall, handsome, slender, but well knit; he seem'd
Active, though not so sprightly, as a page;
   And everybody but his mother deem'd
Him almost man; but she flew in a rage
   And bit her lips (for else she might have scream'd),
If any said so, for to be precocious
Was in her eyes a thing the most atrocious.

LV

Amongst her numerous acquaintance, all
   Selected for discretion and devotion,
There was the Donna Julia, whom to call
   Pretty were but to give a feeble notion

Of many charms in her as natural
　　As sweetness to the flower, or salt to ocean,
Her zone to Venus, or his bow to Cupid,
(But this last simile is trite and stupid).

LVI

The darkness of her oriental eye
　　Accorded with her Moorish origin;
(Her blood was not all Spanish, by the by;
　　In Spain, you know, this is a sort of sin.)
When proud Granada fell, and, forced to fly,
　　Boabdil wept, of Donna Julia's kin
Some went to Africa, some stay'd in Spain,
Her great great grandmamma chose to remain.

LVII

She married (I forget the pedigree)
　　With an Hidalgo, who transmitted down
His blood less noble than such blood should be;
　　At such alliances his sires would frown,
In that point so precise in each degree
　　That they bred *in and in*, as might be shown,
Marrying their cousins—nay, their aunts and nieces,
Which always spoils the breed, if it increases.

LVIII

This heathenish cross restored the breed again,
　　Ruin'd its blood, but much improved its flesh;
For from a root the ugliest in Old Spain
　　Sprung up a branch as beautiful as fresh;
The sons no more were short, the daughters plain:
　　But there's a rumour which I fain would hush,
'Tis that Donna Julia's grandmamma
Produced her Don more heirs at love than law.

LIX

However this might be, the race went on
   Improving still through every generation,
Until it centred in an only son,
   Who left an only daughter; my narration
May have suggested that this single one
   Could be but Julia, (whom on this occasion
I shall have much to speak about), and she
Was married, charming, chaste, and twenty-three.

LX

Her eye (I'm very fond of handsome eyes)
   Was large and dark, suppressing half its fire
Until she spoke, then through its soft disguise
   Flash'd an expression more of pride than ire,
And love than either; and there would arise
   A something in them which was not desire,
But would have been, perhaps, but for the soul
Which struggled through and chasten'd down the whole.

LXI

Her glossy hair was cluster'd o'er a brow
   Bright with intelligence, and fair, and smooth;
Her eyebrow's shape was like the aerial bow,
   Her cheek all purple with the beam of youth,
Mounting, at times, to a transparent glow,
   As if her veins ran lightning; she, in sooth,
Possess'd an air and grace by no means common:
Her stature tall—I hate a dumpy woman.

LXII

Wedded she was some years, and to a man
   Of fifty, and such husbands are in plenty;
And yet, I think, instead of such a ONE
   'Twere better to have TWO of five-and-twenty,

Especially in countries near the sun:
　And now I think on't, 'mi vien in mente',
Ladies even of the most uneasy virtue
Prefer a spouse whose age is short of thirty.

LXIII

'Tis a sad thing, I cannot choose but say,
　And all the fault of that indecent sun,
Who cannot leave alone our helpless clay,
　But will keep baking, broiling, burning on,
That howsoever people fast and pray,
　The flesh is frail, and so the soul undone:
What men call gallantry, and gods adultery,
Is much more common where the climate's sultry. . . .

＊　＊　＊

LXV

Alfonso was the name of Julia's lord,
　A man well looking for his years, and who
Was neither much beloved nor yet abhorr'd;
　They lived together as most people do,
Suffering each other's foibles by accord,
　And not exactly either *one* or *two*;
Yet he was jealous, though he did not show it,
For jealousy dislikes the world to know it.

LXVI

Julia was—yet I never could see why—
　With Donna Inez quite a favourite friend;
Between their tastes there was small sympathy,
　For not a line had Julia ever penn'd:
Some people whisper (but, no doubt, they lie,
　For malice still imputes some private end)
That Inez had, ere Don Alfonso's marriage,
Forgot with him her very prudent carriage;

LXVII

And that still keeping up the old connexion,
  Which time had lately render'd much more chaste,
She took his lady also in affection,
  And certainly this course was much the best:
She flatter'd Julia with her sage protection,
  And complimented Don Alfonso's taste;
And if she could not (who can?) silence scandal,
At least she left it a more slender handle.

LXVIII

I can't tell whether Julia saw the affair
  With other people's eyes, or if her own
Discoveries made, but none could be aware
  Of this, at least no symptom e'er was shown;
Perhaps she did not know, or did not care,
  Indifferent from the first, or callous grown:
I'm really puzzled what to think or say,
  She kept her counsel in so close a way.

LXIX

Juan she saw, and, as a pretty child,
  Caress'd him often—such a thing might be
Quite innocently done, and harmless styled,
  When she had twenty years, and thirteen he;
But I am not so sure I should have smiled
  When he was sixteen, Julia twenty-three;
These few short years make wondrous alterations,
Particularly amongst sun-burnt nations.

LXX

Whate'er the cause might be, they had become
  Changed; for the dame grew distant, the youth shy,
Their looks cast down, their greetings almost dumb,
  And much embarrassment in either eye;

There surely will be little doubt with some
   That Donna Julia knew the reason why,
But as for Juan, he had no more notion
Than he who never saw the sea of ocean.

LXXI

Yet Julia's very coldness still was kind,
   And tremulously gentle her small hand
Withdrew itself from his, but left behind
   A little pressure, thrilling, and so bland
And slight, so very slight, that to the mind
   'Twas but a doubt; but ne'er magician's wand
Wrought change with all Armida's fairy art
Like what this light touch left on Juan's heart.

LXXII

And if she met him, though she smiled no more,
   She look'd a sadness sweeter than her smile,
As if her heart had deeper thoughts in store
   She must not own, but cherish'd more the while
For that compression in its burning core;
   Even innocence itself has many a wile,
And will not dare to trust itself with truth,
And love is taught hypocrisy from youth.

LXXIII

But passion most dissembles, yet betrays
   Even by its darkness; as the blackest sky
Foretells the heaviest tempest, it displays
   Its workings through the vainly guarded eye,
And in whatever aspect it arrays
   Itself, 'tis still the same hypocrisy;
Coldness or anger, even disdain or hate,
Are masks it often wears, and still too late.

LXXIV

Then there were sighs, the deeper for suppression,
  And stolen glances, sweeter for the theft,
And burning blushes, though for no transgression,
  Tremblings when met, and restlessness when left;
All these are little preludes to possession,
  Of which young passion cannot be bereft,
And merely tend to show how greatly love is
Embarrass'd at first starting with a novice.

LXXV

Poor Julia's heart was in an awkward state;
  She felt it going, and resolved to make
The noblest efforts for herself and mate,
  For honour's, pride's, religion's, virtue's sake.
Her resolutions were most truly great,
  And almost might have made a Tarquin quake;
She pray'd the Virgin Mary for her grace,
As being the best judge of a lady's case.

LXXVI

She vow'd she never would see Juan more,
  And next day paid a visit to his mother,
And look'd extremely at the opening door,
  Which, by the Virgin's grace, let in another;
Grateful she was, and yet a little sore—
  Again it opens, it can be no other,
'Tis surely Juan now—No! I'm afraid
That night the Virgin was no further pray'd.

LXXVII

She now determined that a virtuous woman
  Should rather face and overcome temptation,
That flight was base and dastardly, and no man
  Should ever give her heart the least sensation;

That is to say, a thought beyond the common
　　Preference, that we must feel upon occasion,
For people who are pleasanter than others,
But then they only seem so many brothers. . . .

* 　 * 　 *

LXXXI

Love, then, but love within its proper limits,
　　Was Julia's innocent determination
In young Don Juan's favour, and to him its
　　Exertion might be useful on occasion;
And, lighted at too pure a shrine to dim its
　　Ethereal lustre, with what sweet persuasion
He might be taught, by love and her together—
I really don't know what, nor Julia either.

LXXXII

Fraught with this fine intention, and well fenced
　　In mail of proof—her purity of soul,
She, for the future of her strength convinced,
　　And that her honour was a rock, or mole,
Exceeding sagely from that hour dispensed
　　With any kind of troublesome control;
But whether Julia to the task was equal
Is that which must be mention'd in the sequel.

LXXXIII

Her plan she deem'd both innocent and feasible,
　　And, surely, with a stripling of sixteen
Not scandal's fangs could fix on much that's seizable,
　　Or if they did so, satisfied to mean
Nothing but what was good, her breast was peaceable—
　　A quiet conscience makes one so serene!
Christians have burnt each other, quite persuaded
That all the Apostles would have done as they did.

LXXXIV

And if in the mean time her husband died,
   But heaven forbid that such a thought should cross
Her brain, though in a dream! (and then she sigh'd)
   Never could she survive that common loss;
But just suppose that moment should betide,
   I only say suppose it—*inter nos*.
(This should be *entre nous*, for Julia thought
In French, but then the rhyme would go for nought.)

LXXXV

I only say, suppose this supposition:
   Juan being then grown up to man's estate
Would fully suit a widow of condition,
   Even seven years hence it would not be too late;
And in the interim (to pursue this vision)
   The mischief, after all, could not be great,
For he would learn the rudiments of love,
I mean the seraph way of those above.

LXXXVI

So much for Julia. Now we'll turn to Juan.
   Poor little fellow! he had no idea
Of his own case, and never hit the true one;
   In feelings quick as Ovid's Miss Medea,
He puzzled over what he found a new one,
   But not as yet imagined it could be a
Thing quite in course, and not at all alarming,
Which, with a little patience, might grow charming.

LXXXVII

Silent and pensive, idle, restless, slow,
   His home deserted for the lonely wood,
Tormented with a wound he could not know,
   His, like all deep grief, plunged in solitude:

I'm fond myself of solitude or so,
   But then, I beg it may be understood,
By solitude I mean a sultan's, not
A hermit's, with a haram for a grot. . . .

           *   *   *

XC

Young Juan wander'd by the glassy brooks,
   Thinking unutterable things; he threw
Himself at length within the leafy nooks
   Where the wild branch of the cork forest grew;
There poets find materials for their books,
   And every now and then we ready them through,
So that their plan and prosody are eligible,
Unless, like Wordsworth, they prove unintelligible.

XCI

He, Juan (and not Wordsworth), so pursued
   His self-communion with his own high soul,
Until his mighty heart, in its great mood,
   Had mitigated part, though not the whole
Of its disease; he did the best he could
   With things not very subject to control,
And turn'd, without perceiving his condition,
Like Coleridge, into a metaphysician.

XCII

He thought about himself, and the whole earth,
   Of man the wonderful, and of the stars,
And how the deuce they ever could have birth;
   And then he thought of earthquakes, and of wars,
How many miles the moon might have in girth,
   Of air-balloons, and of the many bars
To perfect knowledge of the boundless skies;
And then he thought of Donna Julia's eyes.

XCIII

In thoughts like these true wisdom may discern
   Longings sublime, and aspirations high,
Which some are born with, but the most part learn
   To plague themselves withal, they know not why:
'Twas strange that one so young should thus concern
   His brain about the action of the sky;
If *you* think 'twas philosophy that this did,
I can't help thinking puberty assisted. . . .

*   *   *

XCVII

Those lonely walks, and lengthening reveries,
   Could not escape the gentle Julia's eyes;
She saw that Juan was not at his ease;
   But that which chiefly may, and must surprise,
Is, that the Donna Inez did not tease
   Her only son with question or surmise;
Whether it was she did not see, or would not,
Or, like all very clever people, could not. . . .

*   *   *

CII

It was upon a day, a summer's day;—
   Summer's indeed a very dangerous season,
And so is spring about the end of May;
   The sun, no doubt, is the prevailing reason;
But whatsoe'er the cause is, one may say,
   And stand convicted of more truth than treason,
That there are months which nature grows more merry in,
March has its hares, and May must have its heroine.

CIII

'Twas on a summer's day—the sixth of June:—
   I like to be particular in dates,
Not only of the age, and year, but moon;
   They are a sort of post-house, where the Fates
E

Change horses, making history change its tune,
    Then spur away o'er empires and o'er states,
Leaving at last not much besides chronology,
Excepting the post-obits of theology.

CIV

'Twas on the sixth of June, about the hour
    Of half-past six—perhaps still nearer seven—
When Julia sate within as pretty a bower
    As e'er held houri in that heathenish heaven
Described by Mahomet, and Anacreon Moore,
    To whom the lyre and laurels have geen given,
With all the trophies of triumphant song—
He won them well, and may he wear them long!

CV

She sate, but not alone; I know not well
    How this same interview had taken place,
And even if I knew, I should not tell!—
    People should hold their tongues in any case;
No matter how or why the thing befell,
    But there were she and Juan, face to face—
When two such faces are so, 'twould be wise,
But very difficult, to shut their eyes.

CVI

How beautiful she look'd! her conscious heart
    Glow'd in her cheek, and yet she felt no wrong.
Oh Love! how perfect is thy mystic art,
    Strengthening the weak, and trampling on the strong!
How self-deceitful is the sagest part
    Of mortals whom thy lure hath led along!—
The precipice she stood on was immense,
So was her creed in her own innocence.

CVII

She thought of her own strength, and Juan's youth,
    And of the folly of all prudish fears,
Victorious virtue, and domestic truth,
    And then of Don Alfonso's fifty years:
I wish these last had not occurr'd, in sooth,
    Because that number rarely much endears,
And through all climes, the snowy and the sunny,
Sounds ill in love, whate'er it may in money.

CVIII

When people say, 'I've told you *fifty* times',
    They mean to scold, and very often do;
When poets say, 'I've written *fifty* rhymes',
    They make you dread that they'll recite them too;
In gangs of *fifty*, thieves commit their crimes;
    At *fifty* love for love is rare, 'tis true,
But then, no doubt, it equally as true is,
A good deal may be bought for *fifty* Louis.

CIX

Julia had honour, virtue, truth, and love
    For Don Alfonso; and she inly swore,
By all the vows below to powers above,
    She never would disgrace the ring she wore,
Nor leave a wish which wisdom might reprove;
    And while she ponder'd this, besides much more,
One hand on Juan's carelessly was thrown,
Quite by mistake—she thought it was her own;

CX

Unconsciously she lean'd upon the other,
    Which play'd within the tangles of her hair;
And to contend with thoughts she could not smother
    She seem'd, by the distraction of her air.

'Twas surely very wrong in Juan's mother
　To leave together this imprudent pair,
She who for many years had watch'd her son so—
I'm very certain *mine* would not have done so.

CXI

The hand which still held Juan's, by degrees
　Gently, but palpably confirm'd its grasp,
As if it said, 'Detain me, if you please;'
　Yet there's no doubt she only meant to clasp
His fingers with a pure Platonic squeeze;
　She would have shrunk as from a toad, or asp,
Had she imagined such a thing could rouse
A feeling dangerous to a prudent spouse.

CXII

I cannot know what Juan thought of this,
　But what he did, is much what you would do;
His young lip thank'd it with a grateful kiss,
　And then, abash'd at its own joy, withdrew
In deep despair, lest he had done amiss,
　Love is so very timid when 'tis new:
She blush'd, and frown'd not, but she strove to speak,
And held her tongue, her voice was grown so weak.

CXIII

The sun set, and up rose the yellow moon:
　The devil's in the moon for mischief; they
Who call'd her CHASTE, methinks, began too soon
　Their nomenclature; there is not a day,
The longest, not the twenty-first of June,
　Sees half the business in a wicked way
On which three single hours of moonshine smile—
And then she looks so modest all the while.

CXIV

There is a dangerous silence in that hour,
  A stillness, which leaves room for the full soul
To open all itself, without the power
  Of calling wholly back its self-control;
The silver light which, hallowing tree and tower,
  Sheds beauty and deep softness o'er the whole,
Breathes also to the heart, and o'er it throws
A loving languor, which is not repose.

CXV

And Julia sate with Juan, half embraced
  And half retiring from the glowing arm,
Which trembled like the bosom where 'twas placed;
  Yet still she must have thought there was no harm
Or else 'twere easy to withdraw her waist;
  But then the situation had its charm,
And then——God knows what next—I can't go on;
I'm almost sorry that I e'er begun.

CXVI

Oh Plato! Plato! you have paved the way,
  With your confounded fantasies, to more
Immoral conduct by the fancied sway
  Your system feigns o'er the controlless core
Of human hearts, than all the long array
  Of poets and romancers:—You're a bore,
A charlatan, a coxcomb—and have been,
At best, no better than a go-between.

CXVII

And Julia's voice was lost, except in sighs,
  Until too late for useful conversation;
The tears were gushing from her gentle eyes,
  I wish, indeed, they had not had occasion;

But who, alas! can love, and then be wise?
  Not that remorse did not oppose temptation;
A little still she strove, and much repented,
And whispering 'I will ne'er consent'—consented. . . .

                    *   *   *

CXX

Here my chaste Muse a liberty must take—
  Start not! still chaster reader—she'll be nice hence-
Forward, and there is no great cause to quake;
  This liberty is a poetic licence,
Which some irregularity may make
  In the design, and as I have a high sense
Of Aristotle and the Rules, 'tis fit
To beg his pardon when I err a bit.

CXXI

This licence is to hope the reader will
  Suppose from June the sixth (the fatal day,
Without whose epoch my poetic skill
  For want of facts would all be thrown away),
But keeping Julia and Don Juan still
  In sight, that several months have pass'd; we'll say
'Twas in November, but I'm not so sure
About the day—the era's more obscure.

CXXII

We'll talk of that anon.—'Tis sweet to hear
  At midnight on the blue and moonlit deep
The song and oar of Adria's gondolier,
  By distance mellow'd, o'er the waters sweep;
'Tis sweet to see the evening star appear;
  'Tis sweet to listen as the night-winds creep
From leaf to leaf; 'tis sweet to view on high
The rainbow, based on ocean, span the sky.

CXXIII

'Tis sweet to hear the watch-dog's honest bark
　　Bay deep-mouth'd welcome as we draw near home;
'Tis sweet to know there is an eye will mark
　　Our coming, and look brighter when we come;
'Tis sweet to be awaken'd by the lark,
　　Or lull'd by falling waters; sweet the hum
Of bees, the voice of girls, the song of birds,
The lisp of children, and their earliest words.

CXXIV

Sweet is the vintage, when the showering grapes
　　In Bacchanal profusion reel to earth
Purple and gushing; sweet are our escapes
　　From civic revelry to rural mirth;
Sweet to the miser are his glittering heaps,
　　Sweet to the father is his first-born's birth,
Sweet is revenge—especially to women,
Pillage to soldiers, prize-money to seamen.

CXXV

Sweet is a legacy, and passing sweet
　　The unexpected death of some old lady
Or gentleman of seventy years complete,
　　Who've made 'us youth' wait too—too long already
For an estate, or cash, or country seat,
　　Still breaking, but with stamina so steady
That all the Israelites are fit to mob its
Next owner for their double-damn'd post-obits.

CXXVI

'Tis sweet to win, no matter how, one's laurels,
　　By blood or ink; 'tis sweet to put an end
To strife; 'tis sometimes sweet to have our quarrels,
　　Particularly with a tiresome friend;

Sweet is old wine in bottles, ale in barrels;
    Dear is the helpless creature we defend
Against the world; and dear the schoolboy spot
We ne'er forget, though there we are forgot.

CXXVII

But sweeter still than this, than these, than all,
    Is first and passionate love—it stands alone,
Like Adam's recollection of his fall;
    The tree of knowledge has been pluck'd—all's
       known—
And life yields nothing further to recall
    Worthy of this ambrosial sin, so shown,
No doubt in fable, as the unforgiven
Fire which Prometheus filch'd for us from heaven. . . .

*   *   *

CXXXIII

Man's a phenomenon, one knows not what,
    And wonderful beyond all wondrous measure;
'Tis a pity though, in this sublime world, that
    Pleasure's a sin, and sometimes sin's a pleasure;
Few mortals know what end they would be at,
    But whether glory, power, or love, or treasure,
The path is through perplexing ways, and when
The goal is gain'd, we die, you know—and then——

CXXXIV

What then?—I do not know, no more do you—
    And so good night.—Return we to our story:
'Twas in November, when fine days are few,
    And the far mountains wax a little hoary,
And clap a white cape on their mantles blue;
    And the sea dashes round the promontory,
And the loud breaker boils against the rock,
And sober suns must set at five o'clock.

CXXXV

'Twas, as the watchmen say, a cloudynight;
   No moon, no stars, the wind was low or loud
By gusts, and many a sparkling hearth was bright
   With the piled wood, round which the family crowd;
There's something cheerful in that sort of light,
   Even as a summer sky's without a cloud:
I'm fond of fire, and crickets, and all that,
A lobster salad, and champagne, and chat.

CXXXVI

'Twas midnight—Donna Julia was in bed,
   Sleeping, most probably,—when at her door
Arose a clatter might awake the dead,
   If they had never been awoke before,
And that they have been so we all have read,
   And are to be so, at the least, once more;—
The door was fasten'd, but with voice and fist
First knocks were heard, then 'Madam—Madam—hist!

CXXXVII

'For God's sake, Madam—Madam—here's my master,
   With more than half the city at his back—
Was ever heard of such a curst disaster!
   'Tis not my fault—I kept good watch—Alack!
Do pray undo the bolt a little faster—
   They're on the stair just now, and in a crack
Will all be here; perhaps he yet may fly—
Surely the window's not so *very* high!'

CXXXVIII

By this time Don Alfonso was arrived,
   With torches, friends, and servants in great number;
The major part of them had long been wived,
   And therefore paused not to disturb the slumber

Of any wicked woman, who contrived
  By stealth her husband's temples to encumber:
Examples of this kind are so contagious,
Were *one* not punish'd, *all* would be outrageous.

CXXXIX

I can't tell how, or why, or what suspicion
  Could enter into Don Alfonso's head;
But for a cavalier of his condition
  It surely was exceedingly ill-bred,
Without a word of previous admonition,
  To hold a levee round his lady's bed,
And summon lackeys, arm'd with fire and sword,
To prove himself the thing he most abhorr'd.

CXL

Poor Donna Julia! starting as from sleep
  (Mind—that I do not say—she had not slept)
Began at once to scream, and yawn, and weep;
  Her maid, Antonia, who was an adept,
Contrived to fling the bed-clothes in a heap,
  As if she had just now from out them crept:
I can't tell why she should take all this trouble
To prove her mistress had been sleeping double.

CXLI

But Julia mistress, and Antonia maid,
  Appear'd like two poor harmless women, who
Of goblins, but still more of men afraid,
  Had thought one man might be deterr'd by two,
And therefore side by side were gently laid,
  Until the hours of absence should run through
And truant husband should return, and say,
'My dear, I was the first who came away.'

CXLII

Now Julia found at length a voice, and cried,
  'In heaven's name, Don Alfonso, what d'ye mean?
Has madness seized you? would that I had died
  Ere such a monster's victim I had been!
What may this midnight violence betide,
  A sudden fit of drunkenness or spleen?
Dare you suspect me, whom the thought would kill?
Search, then, the room!'—Alfonso said, 'I will.'

CXLIII

He search'd, *they* search'd, and rummaged everywhere,
  Closet and clothes-press, chest and window-seat,
And found much linen, lace, and several pair
  Of stockings, slippers, brushes, combs, complete,
With other articles of ladies fair,
  To keep them beautiful, or leave them neat:
Arras they prick'd and curtains with their swords,
And wounded several shutters, and some boards.

CXLIV

Under the bed they search'd, and there they found—
  No matter what—it was not that they sought;
They open'd windows, gazing if the ground
  Had signs or footmarks, but the earth said nought;
And then they stared each other's faces round:
  'Tis odd, not one of all these seekers thought,
And seems to me almost a sort of blunder,
Of looking *in* the bed as well as under.

CXLV

During this inquisition Julia's tongue
  Was not asleep—'Yes, search and search,' she cried,
'Insult on insult heap, and wrong on wrong!
  It was for this that I became a bride!

For this in silence I have suffer'd long
　　A husband like Alfonso at my side;
But now I'll bear no more, nor here remain,
If there be law, or lawyers, in all Spain.

CXLVI

'Yes, Don Alfonso! husband now no more,
　　If ever you indeed deserved the name,
　Is't worthy of your years?—you have three-score—
　　Fifty, or sixty, it is all the same—
Is't wise or fitting causeless to explore
　　For facts against a virtuous woman's fame?
Ungrateful, perjured, barbarous Don Alfonso,
How dare you think your lady would go on so? . . .

*　　*　　*

CLIII

'There is the closet, there the toilet, there
　　The antechamber—search them under, over;
There is the sofa, there the great arm-chair,
　　The chimney—which would really hold a lover.
I wish to sleep, and beg you will take care
　　And make no further noise, till you discover
The secret cavern of this lurking treasure—
And when 'tis found, let me, too, have that pleasure.

CLIV

'And now, Hidalgo! now that you have thrown
　　Doubt upon me, confusion over all,
Pray have the courtesy to make it known
　　Who is the man you search for? how d'ye call
Him? what's his lineage? let him but be shown—
　　I hope he's young and handsome—is he tall?
Tell me—and be assured, that since you stain
Mine honour thus, it shall not be in vain.

CLV

'At least, perhaps, he has not sixty years,
    At that age he would be too old for slaughter,
Or for so young a husband's jealous fears—
    (Antonia! let me have a glass of water.)
I am ashamed of having shed these tears,
    They are unworthy of my father's daughter;
My mother dream'd not in my natal hour,
That I should fall into a monster's power.

CLVI

'Perhaps 'tis of Antonia you are jealous,
    You saw that she was sleeping by my side,
When you broke in upon us with your fellows:
    Look where you please—we've nothing, sir, to hide;
Only another time, I trust, you'll tell us,
    Or for the sake of decency abide
A moment at the door, that we may be
Drest to receive so much good company.

CLVII

'And now, sir, I have done, and say no more;
    The little I have said may serve to show
The guileless heart in silence may grieve o'er
    The wrongs to whose exposure it is slow:—
I leave you to your conscience as before,
    'Twill one day ask you, *why* you used me so?
God grant you feel not then the bitterest grief!
Antonia! where's my pocket-handkerchief?'

CLVIII

She ceased, and turn'd upon her pillow; pale
    She lay, her dark eyes flashing through their tears,
Like skies that rain and lighten; as a veil,
    Waved and o'ershading her wan cheek, appears

Her streaming hair; the black curls strive, but fail,
    To hide the glossy shoulder, which uprears
Its snow through all;—her soft lips lie apart,
And louder than her breathing beats her heart.

CLIX

The Senhor Don Alfonso stood confused;
    Antonia bustled round the ransack'd room,
And, turning up her nose, with looks abused
    Her master, and his myrmidons, of whom
Not one, except the attorney, was amused;
    He, like Achates, faithful to the tomb,
So there were quarrels, cared not for the cause,
Knowing they must be settled by the laws.

CLX

With prying snub-nose, and small eyes, he stood,
    Following Antonia's motions here and there,
With much suspicion in his attitude;
    For reputations he had little care;
So that a suit or action were made good,
    Small pity had he for the young and fair,
And ne'er believed in negatives, till these
Were proved by competent false witnesses.

CLXI

But Don Alfonso stood with downcast looks,
    And, truth to say, he made a foolish figure;
When, after searching in five hundred nooks,
    And treating a young wife with so much rigour,
He gain'd no point, except some self-rebukes,
    Added to those his lady with such vigour
Had pour'd upon him for the last half hour,
Quick, thick, and heavy—as a thunder-shower.

CLXII

At first he tried to hammer an excuse,
  To which the sole reply was tears and sobs,
And indication of hysterics, whose
  Prologue is always certain throes, and throbs,
Gasps, and whatever else the owners choose:
  Alfonso saw his wife, and thought of Job's;
He saw too, in perspective, her relations,
And then he tried to muster all his patience.

CLXIII

He stood in act to speak, or rather stammer,
  But sage Antonia cut him short before
The anvil of his speech received the hammer,
  With 'Pray, sir, leave the room, and say no more,
Or madam dies.'—Alfonso mutter'd, 'D—n her,'
  But nothing else, the time of words was o'er;
He cast a rueful look or two, and did,
He knew not wherefore, that which he was bid.

CLXIV

With him retired his *'posse comitatus'*,
  The attorney last, who linger'd near the door,
Reluctantly, still tarrying there as late as
  Antonia let him—not a little sore
At this most strange and unexplain'd *'hiatus'*
  In Don Alfonso's facts, which just now wore
An awkward look; as he revolved the case,
The door was fasten'd in his legal face.

CLXV

No sooner was it bolted, than—Oh shame!
  Oh sin! Oh sorrow! and Oh womankind!
How can you do such things and keep your fame,
  Unless this world, and t'other too, be blind?

Nothing so dear as an unfilch'd good name!
　　But to proceed—for there is more behind:
With much heartfelt reluctance be it said,
Young Juan slipp'd, half-smother'd, from the bed.

CLXVI

He had been hid—I don't pretend to say
　　How, nor can I indeed describe the where—
Young, slender, and pack'd easily, he lay,
　　No doubt, in little compass, round or square;
But pity him I neither must nor may
　　His suffocation by that pretty pair;
'Twere better, sure, to die so, than be shut
With maudlin Clarence in his Malmsey butt.

CLXVII

And, secondly, I pity not, because
　　He had no business to commit a sin,
Forbid by heavenly, fined by human laws,
　　At least 'twas rather early to begin;
But at sixteen the conscience rarely gnaws
　　So much as when we call our old debts in
At sixty years, and draw the accompts of evil,
And find a deuced balance with the devil.

CLXVIII

Of his position I can give no notion:
　　'Tis written in the Hebrew Chronicle,
How the physicians, leaving pill and potion,
　　Prescribed, by way of blister, a young belle,
When old King David's blood grew dull in motion,
　　And that the medicine answer'd very well;
Perhaps 'twas in a different way applied,
For David lived, but Juan nearly died.

CLXIX

What's to be done? Alfonso will be back
  The moment he has sent his fools away.
Antonia's skill was put upon the rack,
  But no device could be brought into play—
And how to parry the renew'd attack?
  Besides, it wanted but few hours of day:
Antonia puzzled; Julia did not speak,
But press'd her bloodless lip to Juan's cheek.

CLXX

He turn'd his lip to hers, and with his hand
  Call'd back the tangles of her wandering hair;
Even then their love they could not all command,
  And half forgot their danger and despair:
Antonia's patience now was at a stand—
  'Come, come, 'tis no time now for fooling there,'
She whisper'd, in great wrath—'I must deposit
This pretty gentleman within the closet:

CLXXI

'Pray, keep your nonsense for some luckier night—
  Who can have put my master in this mood?
What will become on't—I'm in such a fright,
  The devil's in the urchin, and no good—
Is this a time for giggling? this a plight?
  Why, don't you know that it may end in blood?
You'll lose your life, and I shall lose my place,
My mistress all, for that half-girlish face.

CLXXII

'Had it but been for a stout cavalier
  Or twenty-five or thirty—(come, make haste)
But for a child, what piece of work is here!
  I really, madam, wonder at your taste—

F

(Come, sir, get in)—my master must be near:
  There, for the present, at the least, he's fast,
And if we can but till the morning keep
  Our counsel—(Juan, mind, you must not sleep).'

CLXXIII

Now, Don Alfonso entering, but alone,
  Closed the oration of the trusty maid:
She loiter'd, and he told her to be gone,
  An order somewhat sullenly obey'd;
However, present remedy was none,
  And no great good seem'd answer'd if she staid;
Regarding both with slow and sidelong view,
She snuff'd the candle, curtsied, and withdrew.

CLXXIV

Alfonso paused a minute—then begun
  Some strange excuses for his late proceeding;
He would not justify what he had done,
  To say the best, it was extreme ill-breeding;
But there were ample reasons for it, none
  Of which he specified in this his pleading:
His speech was a fine sample, on the whole,
Of rhetoric, which the learn'd call '*rigmarole*'.

CLXXV

Julia said nought; though all the while there rose
  A ready answer, which at once enables
A matron, who her husband's foible knows,
  By a few timely words to turn the tables,
Which, if it does not silence, still must pose,
  Even if it should comprise a pack of fables;
'Tis to retort with firmness, and when he
Suspects with *one*, do you reproach with *three*.

CLXXVI

Julia, in fact, had tolerable grounds,—
    Alfonso's loves with Inez were well known;
But whether 'twas that one's own guilt confounds—
    But that can't be, as has been often shown,
A lady with apologies abounds;—
    It might be that her silence sprang alone
From delicacy to Don Juan's ear,
To whom she knew his mother's fame was dear.

CLXXVII

There might be one more motive, which makes two,
    Alfonso ne'er to Juan had alluded,—
Mentioned his jealousy, but never who
    Had been the happy lover, he concluded,
Conceal'd amongst his premises; 'tis true,
    His mind the more o'er this its mystery brooded;
To speak of Inez now were, one may say,
Like throwing Juan in Alfonso's way.

CLXXVIII

A hint, in tender cases, is enough;
    Silence is best: besides there is a *tact*
(That modern phrase appears to me sad stuff,
    But it will serve to keep my verse compact)
Which keeps, when push'd by questions rather rough,
    A lady always distant from the fact:
The charming creatures lie with such a grace,
There's nothing so becoming to the face.

CLXXIX

They blush, and we believe them; at least I
    Have always done so; 'tis of no great use,
In any case, attempting a reply,
    For then their eloquence grows quite profuse;

And when at length they're out of breath, they sigh,
   And cast their languid eyes down, and let loose
A tear or two, and then we make it up;
And then—and then—and then—sit down and sup.

CLXXX

Alfonso closed his speech, and begg'd her pardon,
   Which Julia half withheld, and then half granted.
And laid conditions, he thought very hard, on,
   Denying several little things he wanted:
He stood like Adam lingering near his garden,
   With useless penitence perplex'd and haunted,
Beseeching she no further would refuse,
When, lo! he stumbled o'er a pair of shoes.

CLXXXI

A pair of shoes!—what then? not much, if they
   Are such as fit with ladies' feet, but these
(No one can tell how much I grieve to say)
   Were masculine; to see them, and to seize,
Was but a moment's act.—Ah! Well-a-day!
   My teeth begin to chatter, my veins freeze—
Alfonso first examined well their fashion,
And then flew out into another passion.

CLXXXII

He left the room for his relinquish'd sword,
   And Julia instant to the closet flew.
'Fly, Juan, fly! for heaven's sake—not a word—
   The door is open—you may yet slip through
The passage you so often have explored—
   Here is the garden-key—Fly—fly—Adieu!
Haste—haste! I hear Alfonso's hurrying feet—
Day has not broke—there's no one in the street.'

CLXXXIII

None can say that this was not good advice,
   The only mischief was, it came too late;
Of all experience 'tis the usual price,
   A sort of income-tax laid on by fate:
Juan had reach'd the room-door in a trice,
   And might have done so by the garden-gate,
But met Alfonso in his dressing-gown,
Who threaten'd death—so Juan knock'd him down.

CLXXXIV

Dire was the scuffle, and out went the light;
   Antonia cried out 'Rape!' and Julia 'Fire!'
But not a servant stirr'd to aid the fight.
   Alfonso, pommell'd to his heart's desire,
Swore lustily he'd be revenged this night;
   And Juan, too, blasphemed an octave higher;
His blood was up; though young, he was a Tartar,
And not at all disposed to prove a martyr.

CLXXXV

Alfonso's sword had dropp'd ere he could draw it,
   And they continued battling hand to hand,
For Juan very luckily ne'er saw it;
   His temper not being under great command,
If at that moment he had chanced to claw it,
   Alfonso's days had not been in the land
Much longer.—Think of husbands', lovers' lives!
And how ye may be doubly widows—wives!

CLXXXVI

Alfonso grappled to detain the foe,
   And Juan throttled him to get away,
And blood ('twas from the nose) began to flow;
   At last, as they more faintly wrestling lay,

Juan contrived to give an awkward blow,
  And then his only garment quite gave way;
He fled, like Joseph, leaving it; but there,
I doubt, all likeness ends between the pair.

CLXXXVII

Lights came at length, and men, and maids, who found
  An awkward spectacle their eyes before;
Antonia in hysterics, Julia swoon'd,
  Alfonso leaning, breathless, by the door;
Some half-torn drapery scatter'd on the ground,
  Some blood, and several footsteps, but no more:
Juan the gate gain'd, turn'd the key about,
And liking not the inside, lock'd the out.

CLXXXVIII

Here ends this canto.—Need I sing, or say,
  How Juan, naked, favour'd by the night,
Who favours what she should not, found his way,
  And reach'd his home in an unseemly plight?
The pleasant scandal which arose next day,
  The nine days' wonder which was brought to light,
And how Alfonso sued for a divorce,
Were in the English newspapers, of course.

CLXXXIX

If you would like to see the whole proceedings,
  The depositions, and the cause at full,
The names of all the witnesses, the pleadings
  Of counsel to nonsuit, or to annul,
There's more than one edition, and the readings
  Are various, but they none of them are dull;
The best is that in short-hand ta'en by Gurney,
Who to Madrid on purpose made a journey.

CXC

But Donna Inez, to divert the train
    Of one of the most circulating scandals
That had for centuries been known in Spain,
    At least since the retirement of the Vandals,
First vow'd (and never had she vow'd in vain)
    To Virgin Mary several pounds of candles;
And then, by the advice of some old ladies,
She sent her son to be shipp'd off from Cadiz.

CXCI

She had resolved that he should travel through
    All European climes, by land or sea,
To mend his former morals, and get new,
    Especially in France and Italy
(At least this is the thing most people do).
    Julia was sent into a convent; she
Grieved, but, perhaps, her feelings may be better
Shown in the following copy of her Letter:—

CXCII

'They tell me 'tis decided you depart:
    'Tis wise—'tis well, but not the less a pain;
I have no further claim on your young heart,
    Mine is the victim, and would be again;
To love too much has been the only art
    I used;—I write in haste, and if a stain
Be on this sheet, 'tis not what it appears;
My eyeballs burn and throb, but have no tears.

CXCIII

'I loved, I love you, for this love have lost
    State, station, heaven, mankind's, my own esteem,
And yet cannot regret what it hath cost,
    So dear is still the memory of that dream;

Yet, if I name my guilt, 'tis not to boast,
  None can deem harshlier of me than I deem
I trace this scrawl because I cannot rest—
I've nothing to reproach, or to request.

CXCIV

'Man's love is of man's life a thing apart,
  'Tis woman's whole existence; man may range
The court, camp, church, the vessel, and the mart;
  Sword, gown, gain, glory, offer in exchange
Pride, fame, ambition, to fill up his heart,
  And few there are whom these cannot estrange;
Men have all these resources, we but one,
To love again, and be again undone.

CXCV

'You will proceed in pleasure, and in pride,
  Beloved and loving many; all is o'er
For me on earth, except some years to hide
  My shame and sorrow deep in my heart's core;
These I could bear, but cannot cast aside
  The passion which still rages as before,—
And so farewell—forgive me, love me—No,
That word is idle now—but let it go.

CXCVI

'My breast has been all weakness, is so yet;
  But still I think I can collect my mind;
My blood still rushes where my spirit's set,
  As roll the waves before the settled wind;
My heart is feminine, nor can forget—
  To all, except one image, madly blind;
So shakes the needle, and so stands the pole,
As vibrates my fond heart to my fix'd soul.

CXCVII

'I have no more to say, but linger still,
  And dare not set my seal upon this sheet,
And yet I may as well the task fulfil,
  My misery can scarce be more complete:
I had not lived till now, could sorrow kill;
  Death shuns the wretch who fain the blow would meet,
And I must even survive this last adieu,
And bear with life, to love and pray for you!'

CXCVIII

This note was written upon gilt-edged paper
  With a neat little crow-quill, slight and new;
Her small white hand could hardly reach the taper,
  It trembled as magnetic needles do,
And yet she did not let one tear escape her;
  The seal a sun-flower; '*Elle vous suit partout,*'
The motto, cut upon a white cornelian;
The wax was superfine, its hue vermilion.

CXCIX

This was Don Juan's earliest scrape; but whether
  I shall proceed with his adventures is
Dependent on the public altogether;
  We'll see, however, what they say to this,
Their favour in an author's cap's a feather,
  And no great mischief's done by their caprice;
And if their approbation we experience,
Perhaps they'll have some more about a year hence.

CC

My poem's epic, and is meant to be
Divided in twelve books; each book containing,
With love, and war, a heavy gale at sea,
  A list of ships, and captains, and kings reigning,

New characters; the episodes are three:
　　A panorama view of hell's in training,
After the style of Virgil and of Homer,
So that my name of Epic's no misnomer.

CCI

All these things will be specified in time,
　　With strict regard to Aristotle's rules,
The *vade mecum* of the true sublime,
　　Which makes so many poets, and some fools;
Prose poets like blank-verse, I'm fond of rhyme,
　　Good workmen never quarrel with their tools;
I've got new mythological machinery,
And very handsome supernatural scenery.

CCII

There's only one slight difference between
　　Me and my epic brethren gone before,
And here the advantage is my own, I ween
　　(Not that I have not several merits more,
But this will more peculiarly be seen);
　　They so embellish, that 'tis quite a bore
Their labyrinth of fables to thread through,
Whereas this story's actually true.

CCIII

If any person doubt it, I appeal
　　To history, tradition, and to facts,
To newspapers, whose truth all know and feel,
　　To plays in five, and operas in three acts;
All these confirm my statement a good deal,
　　But that which more completely faith exacts
Is, that myself, and several now in Seville,
Saw Juan's last elopement with the devil.

CCIV

If ever I should condescend to prose,
    I'll write poetical commandments, which
Shall supersede beyond all doubt all those
    That went before; in these I shall enrich
My text with many things that no one knows,
    And carry precept to the highest pitch:
I'lll call the work 'Longinus o'er a Bottle,
Or, Every Poet his *own* Aristotle.'

CCV

Thou shalt believe in Milton, Dryden, Pope;
Thou shalt not set up Wordsworth, Coleridge, Southey;
Because the first is crazed beyond all hope,
    The second drunk, the third so quaint and mouthy:
With Crabbe it may be difficult to cope,
    And Campbell's Hippocrene is somewhat drouthy:
Thou shalt not steal from Samuel Rogers, nor
Commit—flirtation with the muse of Moore.

CCVI

Thou shalt not covet Mr. Sotheby's Muse,
    His Pegasus, nor anything that's his;
Thou shalt not bear false witness like 'the Blues'
    (There's one, at least, is very fond of this);
Thou shalt not write, in short, but what I choose:
    This is true criticism, and you may kiss—
Exactly as you please, or not—the rod;
But if you don't, I'll lay it on, by G—d!

CCVII

If any person should presume to assert
    This story is not moral, first, I pray,
That they will not cry out before they're hurt,
    Then that they'll read it o'er again, and say

(But, doubtless, nobody will be so pert),
　　That this is not a moral tale, though gay;
Besides, in Canto Twelfth, I mean to show
The very place where wicked people go.

CCVIII

If, after all, there should be some so blind
　　To their own good this warning to despise,
Let by some tortuosity of mind,
　　Not to believe my verse and their own eyes,
And cry that they 'the moral cannot find',
　　I tell him, if a clergyman, he lies;
Should captains the remark, or critics, make,
They also lie too—under a mistake.

CCIX

The public approbation I expect,
　　And beg they'll take my word about the moral,
Which I with their amusement will connect
　　(So children cutting teeth receive a coral);
Meantime they'll doubtless please to recollect
　　My epical pretensions to the laurel:
For fear some prudish readers should grow skittish,
I've bribed my grandmother's review—the British. . . .

* * *

CCXXII

'Go, little book, from this my solitude!
　　I cast thee on the waters—go thy ways!
And if, as I believe, thy vein be good,
　　The world will find thee after many days.'
When Southey's read, and Wordsworth understood,
　　I can't help putting in my claim to praise—
The four first rhymes are Southey's, every line:
For God's sake, reader! take them not for mine!

CANTO II

I

Oh ye! who teach the ingenuous youth of nations,
  Holland, France, England, Germany, or Spain,
I pray ye flog them upon all occasions,
  It mends their morals, never mind the pain:
The best of mothers and of educations
  In Juan's case were but employ'd in vain,
Since, in a way that's rather of the oddest, he
Became divested of his native modesty.

II

Had he but been placed at a public school,
  In the third form, or even in the fourth,
His daily task had kept his fancy cool,
  At least, had he been nurtured in the north;
Spain may prove an exception to the rule,
  But then exceptions always prove its worth—
A lad of sixteen causing a divorce
Puzzled his tutors very much, of course.

III

I can't say that it puzzles me at all,
  If all things be consider'd; first, there was
His lady-mother, mathematical,
  A —— never mind; his tutor, an old ass;
A pretty woman—(that's quite natural,
  Or else the thing had hardly come to pass);
A husband rather old, not much in unity
With his young wife—a time, and opportunity.

IV

Well—well, the world must turn upon its axis,
   And all mankind turn with it, heads or tails,
And live and die, make love and pay our taxes,
   And as the veering wind shifts, shift our sails;
The king commands us, and the doctor quacks us,
   The priest instructs, and so our life exhales,
A little breath, love, wine, ambition, fame,
Fighting, devotion, dust,—perhaps a name.

V

I said, that Juan had been sent to Cadiz—
   A pretty town, I recollect it well—
'Tis there the mart of the colonial trade is
   (Or was, before Peru learn'd to rebel),
And such sweet girls—I mean, such graceful ladies,
   Their very walk would make your bosom swell;
I can't describe it, though so much it strike,
Nor liken it—I never saw the like. . . .

*   *   *

VIII

But to our tale: the Donna Inez sent
   Her son to Cadiz only to embark;
To stay there had not answer'd her intent,
   But why?—we leave the reader in the dark—
'Twas for a voyage the young man was meant,
   As if a Spanish ship were Noah's ark,
To wean him from the wickedness of earth,
And send him like a dove of promise forth.

IX

Don Juan bade his valet pack his things
   According to direction, then received
A lecture and some money: for four springs
   He was to travel; and though Inez grieved

(As every kind of parting has its stings),
   She hoped he would improve—perhaps believed:
A letter, too, she gave (he never read it)
Of good advice—and two or three of credit.

                         X

In the mean time, to pass her hours away,
   Brave Inez now set up a Sunday school
For naughty children, who would rather play
   (Like truant rogues) the devil, or the fool;
Infants of three years old were taught that day,
   Dunces were whipt, or set upon a stool:
The great success of Juan's education
Spurr'd her to teach another generation.

                        XI

Juan embark'd—the ship got under way,
   The wind was fair, the water passing rough;
A devil of a sea rolls in that Bay,
   As I, who've cross'd it oft, know well enough;
And, standing upon deck, the dashing spray
   Flies in one's face, and makes it weather-tough:
And there he stood to take, and take again,
His first—perhaps his last—farewell of Spain.

                        XII

I can't but say it is an awkward sight
   To see one's native land receding through
The growing waters; it unmans one quite,
   Especially when life is rather new:
I recollect Great Britain's coast looks white,
   But almost every other country's blue,
When gazing on them, mystified by distance,
We enter on our nautical existence.

XIII

So Juan stood, bewilder'd, on the deck:
   The wind sung, cordage strain'd, and sailors swore,
And the ship creak'd, the town became a speck,
   From which away so fair and fast they bore.
The best of remedies is a beef-steak
   Against sea-sickness: try it, sir, before
You sneer, and I assure you this is true,
For I have found it answer—so may you.

XIV

Don Juan stood, and, gazing from the stern,
   Beheld his native Spain receding far:
First partings form a lesson hard to learn,
   Even nations feel this when they go to war;
There is a sort of unexprest concern,
   A kind of shock that sets one's heart ajar:
At leaving even the most unpleasant people
And places, one keeps looking at the steeple.

XV

But Juan had got many things to leave,
   His mother, and a mistress, and no wife,
So that he had much better cause to grieve
   Than many persons more advanced in life;
And if we now and then a sigh must heave
   At quitting even those we quit in strife,
No doubt we weep for those the heart endears—
That is, till deeper griefs congeal our tears.

XVI

So Juan wept, as wept the captive Jews
   By Babel's waters, still remembering Sion:
I'd weep,—but mine is not a weeping Muse,
   And such light griefs are not a thing to die on;

Young men should travel, if but to amuse
    Themselves; and the next time their servants tie on
Behind their carriages their new portmanteau,
Perhaps it may be lined with this my canto.

XVII

And Juan wept, and much be sigh'd and thought,
    While his salt tears dropp'd into the salt sea,
'Sweets to the sweet' (I like so much to quote;
    You must excuse this extract,—'tis where she,
The Queen of Denmark, for Ophelia brought
    Flowers to the grave); and, sobbing often, he
Reflected on his present situation,
And seriously resolved on reformation.

XVIII

'Farewell, my Spain! a long farewell!' he cried,
    'Perhaps I may revisit thee no more,
But die, as many an exiled heart hath died,
    Of its own thirst to see again thy shore:
Farewell, where Guadalquivir's waters glide!
    Farewell, my mother! and, since all is o'er,
Farewell, too, dearest Julia!'—(here he drew
Her letter out again, and read it through.)

XIX

'And oh! if e'er I should forget, I swear—
    But that's impossible, and cannot be—
Sooner shall this blue ocean melt to air,
    Sooner shall earth resolve itself to sea,
Than I resign thine image, oh, my fair!
    Or think of anything, excepting thee;
A mind diseased no remedy can physic—'
(Here the ship gave a lurch, and he grew sea-sick.)
G

XX

'Sooner shall heaven kiss earth—' (here he fell sicker)
  'Oh, Julia! what is every other woe?—
(For God's sake let me have a glass of liquor;
  Pedro, Battista, help me down below.)
Julia, my love—(you rascal, Pedro, quicker)—
  Oh, Julia!—(this curst vessel pitches so)—
Beloved Julia, hear me still beseeching!'
(Here he grew inarticulate with retching.)

XXI

He felt that chilling heaviness of heart,
  Or rather stomach, which, alas! attends,
Beyond the best apothecary's art,
  The loss of love, the treachery of friends,
Or death of those we dote on, when a part
  Of us dies with them as each fond hope ends:
No doubt he would have been much more pathetic,
But the sea acted as a strong emetic. . . .

*   *   *

XXIV

The ship, call'd the most holy 'Trinidada',
  Was steering duly for the port Leghorn;
For there the Spanish family Moncada
  Were settled long ere Juan's sire was born:
They were relations, and for them he had a
  Letter of introduction, which the morn
Of his departure had been sent him by
His Spanish friends for those in Italy.

XXV

His suite consisted of three servants and
  A tutor, the licentiate Pedrillo,
Who several languages did understand,
  But now lay sick and speechless on his pillow,

And, rocking in his hammock, long'd for land,
  His headache being increased by every billow;
And the waves oozing through the port-hole made
His berth a little damp, and him afraid.

XXVI

'Twas not without some reason, for the wind
  Increased at night, until it blew a gale;
And though 'twas not much to a naval mind,
  Some landsmen would have look'd a little pale,
For sailors are, in fact, a different kind:
  At sunset they began to take in sail,
For the sky show'd it would come on to blow,
And carry away, perhaps, a mast or so.

XXVII

At one o'clock the wind with sudden shift
  Threw the ship right into the trough of the sea,
Which struck her aft, and made an awkward rift,
  Started the stern-post, also shatter'd the
Whole of her stern-frame, and, ere she could lift
  Herself from out her present jeopardy,
The rudder tore away: 'twas time to sound
The pumps, and there were four feet water found. . . .

*   *   *

XXXIII

It may be easily supposed, while this
  Was going on, some people were unquiet,
That passengers would find it much amiss
  To lose their lives, as well as spoil their diet;
That even the able seaman, deeming his
  Days nearly o'er, might be disposed to riot,
As upon such occasions tars will ask
For grog, and sometimes drink rum from the cask.

XXXIV

There's nought, no doubt, so much the spirit calms
　　As rum and true religion; thus it was,
Some plunder'd, some drank spirits, some sung psalms,
　　The high wind made the treble, and as bass
The hoarse harsh waves kept time; fright cured the
　　　　qualms
Of all the luckless landsmen's sea-sick maws:
Strange sounds of wailing, blasphemy, devotion,
Clamour'd in chorus to the roaring ocean.

XXXV

Perhaps more mischief had been done, but for
　　Our Juan, who, with sense beyond his years,
Got to the spirit-room, and stood before
　　It with a pair of pistols; and their fears,
As if Death were more dreadful by his door
　　Of fire than water, spite of oaths and tears,
Kept still aloof the crew, who, ere they sunk,
Thought it would be becoming to die drunk.

XXXVI

'Give us more grog,' they cried, 'for it will be
　　All one an hour hence.' Juan answer'd, 'No!
'Tis true that death awaits both you and me,
　　But let us die like men, not sink below
Like brutes:'—and thus his dangerous post kept he,
　　And none liked to anticipate the blow;
And even Pedrillo, his most reverend tutor,
Was for some rum a disappointed suitor.

XXXVII

The good old gentleman was quite aghast,
　　And made a loud and pious lamentation;
Repented all his sins, and made a last
　　Irrevocable vow of reformation;

Nothing should tempt him more (this peril past)
    To quit his academic occupation,
In cloisters of the classic Salamanca,
To follow Juan's wake, like Sancho Panca.

XXXVIII

But now there came a flash of hope once more;
    Day broke, and the wind lull'd: the masts were gone;
The leak increased; shoals round her, but no shore,
    The vessel swam, yet still she held her own.
They tried the pumps again, and though before
    Their desperate efforts seem'd all useless grown,
A glimpse of sunshine set some hands to bale—
The stronger pump'd, the weaker thrumm'd a sail. . . .

*   *   *

XLIV

The ship was evidently settling now
    Fast by the head; and, all distinction gone,
Some went to prayers again, and made a vow
    Of candles to their saints—but there were none
To pay them with; and some look'd o'er the bow;
    Some hoisted out the boats; and there was one
That begg'd Pedrillo for an absolution,
Who told him to be damn'd—in his confusion.

XLV

Some lash'd them in their hammocks; some put on
    Their best clothes, as if going to a fair;
Some cursed the day on which they saw the sun,
    And gnash'd their teeth, and, howling, tore their hair;
And others went on as they had begun,
    Getting the boats out, being well aware
That a tight boat will live in a rough sea,
Unless with breakers close beneath her lee.

XLVI

The worst of all was, that in their condition,
  Having been several days in great distress,
'Twas difficult to get out such provision
  As now might render their long suffering less:
Men, even when dying, dislike inanition;
  Their stock was damaged by the weather's stress:
Two casks of biscuit, and a keg of butter,
Were all that could be thrown into the cutter.

XLVII

But in the long-boat they contrived to stow
  Some pounds of bread, though injured by the wet;
Water, a twenty-gallon cask or so;
  Six flasks of wine; and they contrived to get
A portion of their beef up from below,
  And with a piece of pork, moreover, met,
But scarce enough to serve them for a luncheon—
Then there was rum, eight gallons in a puncheon.

XLVIII

The other boats, the yawl and pinnace, had
  Been stove in the beginning of the gale;
And the long-boat's condition was but bad,
  As there were but two blankets for a sail,
And one oar for a mast, which a young lad
  Threw in by good luck over the ship's rail;
And two boats could not hold, far less be stored,
To save one half the people then on board.

XLIX

'Twas twilight, and the sunless day went down
  Over the waste of waters; like a veil,
Which, if withdrawn, would but disclose the frown
  Of one whose hate is mask'd but to assail.

Thus to their hopeless eyes the night was shown,
  And grimly darkled o'er their faces pale,
And the dim desolate deep: twelve days had Fear
Been their familiar, and now Death was here.

L

Some trial had been making at a raft,
  With little hope in such a rolling sea,
A sort of thing at which one would have laugh'd,
  If any laughter at such times could be,
Unless with people who too much have quaff'd,
  And have a kind of wild and horrid glee,
Half epileptical, and half hysterical:—
Their preservation would have been a miracle.

LI

At half-past eight o'clock, booms, hencoops, spars,
  And all things, for a chance, had been cast loose
That still could keep afloat the struggling tars,
  For yet they strove, although of no great use:
There was no light in heaven but a few stars,
  The boats put off o'ercrowded with their crews;
She gave a heel, and then a lurch to port,
And, going down head foremost—sunk, in short.

LII

Then rose from sea to sky the wild farewell—
  Then shriek'd the timid, and stood still the brave—
Then some leap'd overboard with dreadful yell,
  As eager to anticipate their grave;
And the sea yawn'd around her like a hell,
  And down she suck'd with her the whirling wave,
Like one who grapples with his enemy,
And strives to strangle him before he die.

LIII

And first one universal shriek there rush'd,
  Louder than the loud ocean, like a crash
Of echoing thunder; and then all was hush'd,
  Save the wild wind and the remorseless dash
Of billows; but at intervals there gush'd,
  Accompanied with a convulsive splash,
A solitary shriek, the bubbling cry
Of some strong swimmer in his agony.

LIV

The boats, as stated, had got off before,
  And in them crowded several of the crew;
And yet their present hope was hardly more
  Than what it had been, for so strong it blew
There was slight chance of reaching any shore;
  And then they were too many, though so few—
Nine in the cutter, thirty in the boat,
Were counted in them when they got afloat.

LV

All the rest perish'd; near two hundred souls
  Had left their bodies; and what's worse, alas!
When over Catholics the ocean rolls,
  They must wait several weeks before a mass
Takes off one peck of purgatorial coals,
  Because, till people know what's come to pass,
They won't lay out their money on the dead—
It costs three francs for every mass that's said.

LVI

Juan got into the long-boat, and there
  Contrived to help Pedrillo to a place;
It seem'd as if they had exchanged their care,
  For Juan wore the magisterial face

Which courage gives, while poor Pedrillo's pair
    Of eyes were crying for their owner's case:
Battista, though (a name call'd shortly Tita),
Was lost by getting at some aqua-vita.

LVII

Pedro, his valet, too, he tried to save,
    But the same cause, conducive to his loss,
Left him so drunk, he jump'd into the wave,
    As o'er the cutter's edge he tried to cross,
And so he found a wine-and-watery grave;
    They could not rescue him although so close,
Because the sea ran higher every minute,
And for the boat—the crew kept crowding in it.

LVIII

A small old spaniel—which had been Don Jóse's,
    His father's, whom he loved, as ye may think,
For on such things the memory reposes
    With tenderness—stood howling on the brink,
Knowing (dogs have such intellectual noses!),
    No doubt, the vessel was about to sink;
And Juan caught him up, and ere he stepp'd
Off threw him in, then after him he leap'd.

LIX

He also stuff'd his money where he could
    About his person, and Pedrillo's too,
Who let him do, in fact, whate'er he would,
    Not knowing what himself to say, or do,
As every rising wave his dread renew'd;
    But Juan, trusting they might still get through,
And deeming there were remedies for any ill,
Thus re-embark'd his tutor and his spaniel.

LX

'Twas a rough night, and blew so stiffly yet,
  That the sail was becalm'd between the seas,
Though on the wave's high top too much to set,
  They dared not take it in for all the breeze:
Each sea curl'd o'er the stern, and kept them wet,
  And made them bale without a moment's ease,
So that themselves as well as hopes were damp'd,
And the poor little cutter quickly swamp'd.

LXI

Nine souls more went in her: the long-boat still
  Kept above water, with an oar for mast,
Two blankets stitch'd together, answering ill
  Instead of sail, were to the oar made fast:
Though every wave roll'd menacing to fill,
  And present peril all before surpass'd,
They grieved for those who perish'd with the cutter,
And also for the biscuit-casks and butter.

LXII

The sun rose red and fiery, a sure sign
  Of the continuance of the gale: to run
Before the sea, until it should grow fine,
  Was all that for the present could be done:
A few tea-spoonfuls of their rum and wine
  Were served out to the people, who begun
To faint, and damaged bread wet through the bags,
And most of them had little clothes but rags.

LXIII

They counted thirty, crowded in a space
  Which left scarce room for motion or exertion;
They did their best to modify their case,
  One half sate up, though numb'd with the immersion,

While t'other half were laid down in their place,
   At watch and watch: thus, shivering like the tertian
Ague in its cold fit, they fill'd their boat,
With nothing but the sky for a great coat.

LXIV

'Tis very certain the desire of life
   Prolongs it; this is obvious to physicians,
When patients, neither plagued with friends nor wife,
   Survive through very desperate conditions,
Because they still can hope, nor shines the knife
   Nor shears of Atropos before their visions:
Despair of all recovery spoils longevity,
And makes men's miseries of alarming brevity.

LXV

'Tis said that persons living on annuities
   Are longer lived than others,—God knows why,
Unless to plague the grantors,—yet so true it is,
   That some, I really think, *do* never die;
Of any creditors the worst a Jew it is,
   And *that*'s their mode of furnishing supply:
In my young days they lent me cash that way,
Which I found very troublesome to pay.

LXVI

'Tis thus with people in an open boat,
   They live upon the love of life, and bear
More than can be believed, or even thought,
   And stand like rocks the tempest's wear and tear;
And hardship still has been the sailor's lot,
   Since Noah's ark went cruising here and there;
She had a curious crew as well as cargo,
Like the first old Greek privateer, the Argo.

LXVII

But man is a carnivorous production,
  And must have meals, at least one meal a day;
He cannot live, like woodcocks, upon suction,
  But, like the shark and tiger, must have prey;
Although his anatomical construction
  Bears vegetables, in a grumbling way,
Your labouring people think beyond all question
Beef, veal, and mutton, better for digestion.

LXVIII

And thus it was with this our hapless crew;
  For on the third day there came on a calm,
And though at first their strength it might renew,
  And, lying on their weariness like balm,
Lull'd them like turtles sleeping on the blue
  Of ocean, when they woke they felt a qualm,
And fell all ravenously on their provision,
Instead of hoarding it with due precision.

LXIX

The consequence was easily foreseen—
  They ate up all they had, and drank their wine,
In spite of all remonstrances, and then
  On what, in fact, next day were they to dine?
They hoped the wind would rise, these foolish men!
  And carry them to shore; these hopes were fine,
But as they had but one oar, and that brittle,
It would have been more wise to save their victual.

LXX

The fourth day came, but not a breath of air,
  And Ocean slumber'd like an unwean'd child:
The fifth day, and their boat lay floating there,
  The sea and sky were blue, and clear, and mild—

With their one oar (I wish they had had a pair)
  What could they do? and hunger's rage grew wild:
So Juan's spaniel, spite of his entreating,
Was kill'd, and portion'd out for present eating.

LXXI

On the sixth day they fed upon his hide,
  And Juan, who had still refused, because
The creature was his father's dog that died,
  Now feeling all the vulture in his jaws,
With some remorse received (though first denied)
  As a great favour one of the fore-paws,
Which he divided with Pedrillo, who
Devour'd it, longing for the other too.

LXXII

The seventh day, and no wind—the burning sun
  Blister'd and scorch'd, and, stagnant on the sea,
They lay like carcasses; and hope was none,
  Save in the breeze that came not: savagely
They glared upon each other—all was done,
  Water, and wine, and food,—and you might see
The longings of the cannibal arise
(Although they spoke not) in their wolfish eyes.

LXXIII

At length one whisper'd his companion, who
  Whisper'd another, and thus it went round,
And then into a hoarser murmur grew,
  An ominous, and wild, and desperate sound;
And when his comrade's thought each sufferer knew,
  'Twas but his own, suppress'd till now, he found:
And out they spoke of lots for flesh and blood,
And who should die to be his fellow's food.

LXXIV

But ere they came to this, they that day shared
  Some leathern caps, and what remain'd of shoes;
And then they look'd around them, and despair'd,
  And none to be the sacrifice would choose;
At length the lots were torn up, and prepared,
  But of materials that must shock the Muse—
Having no paper, for the want of better,
They took by force from Juan Julia's letter.

LXXV

Then lots were made, and mark'd, and mix'd, and handed
  In silent horror, and their distribution
Lull'd even the savage hunger which demanded,
  Like the Promethean vulture, this pollution;
None in particular had sought or plann'd it,
  'Twas nature gnaw'd them to this resolution,
By which none were permitted to be neuter—
And the lot fell on Juan's luckless tutor.

LXXVI

He but requested to be bled to death:
  The surgeon had his instruments, and bled
Pedrillo, and so gently ebb'd his breath,
  You hardly could perceive when he was dead.
He died as born, a Catholic in faith,
  Like most in the belief in which they're bred,
And first a little crucifix he kiss'd,
And then held out his jugular and wrist.

LXXVII

The surgeon, as there was no other fee,
  Had his first choice of morsels for his pains;
But being thirstiest at the moment, he
  Preferr'd a draught from the fast-flowing veins:

Part was divided, part thrown in the sea,
    And such things as the entrails and the brains
Regaled two sharks, who follow'd o'er the billow—
The sailors ate the rest of poor Pedrillo.

LXXVIII

The sailors ate him, all save three or four,
    Who were not quite so fond of animal food;
To these was added Juan, who, before
    Refusing his own spaniel, hardly could
Feel now his appetite increased much more;
    'Twas not to be expected that he should,
Even in extremity of their disaster,
Dine with them on his pastor and his master.

LXXIX

'Twas better that he did not; for, in fact,
    The consequence was awful in the extreme;
For they, who were most ravenous in the act,
    Went raging mad—Lord! how they did blaspheme!
And foam, and roll, with strange convulsions rack'd,
    Drinking salt-water like a mountain-stream;
Tearing, and grinning, howling, screeching, swearing,
And, with hyæna-laughter, died despairing. . . .

* * *

LXXXIV

And the same night there fell a shower of rain,
    For which their mouths gaped, like the cracks of earth
When dried to summer dust; till taught by pain,
    Men really know not what good water's worth;
If you had been in Turkey or in Spain,
    Or with a famish'd boat's-crew had your berth,
Or in the desert heard the camel's bell,
You'd wish yourself where Truth is—in a well.

LXXXV

It pour'd down torrents, but they were no richer,
    Until they found a ragged piece of sheet,
Which served them as a sort of spongy pitcher,
    And when they deem'd its moisture was complete,
They wrung it out, and though a thirsty ditcher
    Might not have thought the scanty draught so sweet
As a full pot of porter, to their thinking
They ne'er till now had known the joys of drinking.

LXXXVI

And their baked lips, with many a bloody crack,
    Suck'd in the moisture, which like nectar stream'd;
Their throats were ovens, their swoln tongues were black
    As the rich man's in hell, who vainly scream'd
To beg the beggar, who could not rain back
    A drop of dew, when every drop had seem'd
To taste of heaven.—If this be true, indeed,
Some Christians have a comfortable creed. . . .

*　　*　　*

XCVI

With twilight it again came on to blow,
    But not with violence; the stars shone out,
The boat made way; yet now they were so low,
    They knew not where nor what they were about;
Some fancied they saw land, and some said 'No!'
    The frequent fog-banks gave them cause to doubt—
Some swore that they heard breakers, others guns,
And all mistook about the latter once.

XCVII

As morning broke, the light wind died away,
    When he who had the watch sung out and swore,
If 'twas not land that rose with the sun's ray,
    He wish'd that land he never might see more:

And the rest rubb'd their eyes, and saw a bay,
　Or thought they saw, and shaped their course for shore;
For shore it was, and gradually grew
Distinct, and high, and palpable to view.

XCVIII

And then of these some part burst into tears,
　And others, looking with a stupid stare,
Could not yet separate their hopes from fears,
　And seem'd as if they had no further care;
While a few pray'd—(the first time for some years)—
　And at the bottom of the boat three were
Asleep; they shook they by the hand and head,
And tried to awaken them, but found them dead.

XCIX

The day before, fast sleeping on the water,
　They found a turtle of the hawk's-bill kind,
And by good fortune, gliding softly, caught her,
　Which yielded a day's life, and to their mind
Proved even still a more nutritious matter,
　Because it left encouragement behind:
They thought that in such perils, more than chance
Had sent them this for their deliverance.

C

The land appear'd a high and rocky coast,
　And higher grew the mountains as they drew,
Set by a current, toward it: they were lost
　In various conjectures, for none knew
To what part of the earth they had been tost,
　So changeable had been the winds that blew;
Some thought it was Mount Ætna, some the highlands
Of Candia, Cyprus, Rhodes, or other islands.

H

CI

Meantime the current, with a rising gale,
  Still set them onwards to the welcome shore,
Like Charon's bark of spectres, dull and pale:
  Their living freight was now reduced to four,
And three dead, whom their strength could not avail
  To heave into the deep with those before,
Though the two sharks still follow'd them, and dash'd
The spray into their faces as they splash'd.

CII

Famine, despair, cold, thirst, and heat, had done
  Their work on them by turns, and thinn'd them to
Such things a mother had not known her son
  Amidst the skeletons of that gaunt crew;
By night chill'd, by day scorch'd, thus one by one
  They perish'd, until wither'd to these few,
But chiefly by a species of self-slaughter,
In washing down Pedrillo with salt water.

CIII

As they drew nigh the land, which now was seen
  Unequal in its aspect here and there,
They felt the freshness of its growing green,
  That waved in forest-tops, and smooth'd the air,
And fell upon their glazed eyes like a screen
  From glistening waves, and skies so hot and bare—
Lovely seem'd any object that should sweep
Away the vast, salt, dread, eternal deep.

CIV

The shore look'd wild, without a trace of man,
  And girt by formidable waves; but they
Were mad for land, and thus their course they ran,
  Though right ahead the roaring breakers lay:

A reef between them also now began
   To show its boiling surf and bounding spray,
But finding no place for their landing better,
They ran the boat for shore,—and overset her.

CV

But in his native stream, the Guadalquivir,
   Juan to lave his youthful limbs was wont;
And having learnt to swim in that sweet river,
   Had often turn'd the art to some account:
A better swimmer you could scarce see ever,
   He could, perhaps, have pass'd the Hellespont,
As once (a feat on which ourselves we prided)
Leander, Mr. Ekenhead, and I did.

CVI

So here, though faint, emaciated, and stark,
   He buoy'd his boyish limbs, and strove to ply
With the quick wave, and gain, ere it was dark,
   The beach which lay before him, high and dry:
The greatest danger here was from a shark,
   That carried off his neighbour by the thigh;
As for the other two, they could not swim,
So nobody arrived on shore but him.

CVII

Nor yet had he arrived but for the oar,
   Which, providentially for him, was wash'd
Just as his feeble arms could strike no more,
   And the hard wave o'erwhelm'd him as 'twas dash'd
Within his grasp; he clung to it, and sore
   The waters beat while he thereto was lash'd;
At last, with swimming, wading, scrambling, he
Roll'd on the beach, half senseless, from the sea:

CVIII

There, breathless, with his digging nails he clung
   Fast to the sand, lest the returning wave,
From whose reluctant roar his life he wrung,
   Should suck him back to her insatiate grave:
And there he lay, full length, where he was flung,
   Before the entrance of a cliff-worn cave,
With just enough of life to feel its pain,
And deem that it was saved, perhaps in vain.

CIX

With slow and staggering effort he arose,
   But sunk again upon his bleeding knee
And quivering hand; and then he look'd for those
   Who long had been his mates upon the sea;
But none of them appear'd to share his woes,
   Save one, a corpse, from out the famish'd three,
Who died two days before, and now had found
An unknown barren beach for burial-ground.

CX

And as he gazed, his dizzy brain spun fast,
   And down he sunk; and as he sunk, the sand
Swam round and round, and all his senses pass'd:
   He fell upon his side, and his stretch'd hand
Droop'd dripping on the oar (their jury-mast),
   And, like a wither'd lily, on the land
His slender frame and pallid aspect lay,
As fair a thing as e'er was form'd of clay.

CXI

How long in his damp trance young Juan lay
   He knew not, for the earth was gone for him,
And time had nothing more of night nor day
   For his congealing blood, and senses dim;

And how this heavy faintness pass'd away
   He knew not, till each painful pulse and limb,
And tingling vein, seem'd throbbing back to life,
For Death, though vanquish'd, still retired with strife.

CXII

His eyes he open'd, shut, again unclosed,
   For all was doubt and dizziness; he thought
He still was in the boat, and had but dozed,
   And felt again with his despair o'erwrought,
And wish'd it death in which he had reposed,
   And then once more his feelings back were brought,
And slowly by his swimming eyes was seen
A lovely female face of seventeen.

CXIII

'Twas bending close o'er his, and the small mouth
   Seem'd almost prying into his for breath;
And chafing him, the soft warm hand of youth
   Recall'd his answering spirits back from death;
And, bathing his chill temples, tried to soothe
   Each pulse to animation, till beneath
Its gentle touch and trembling care, a sigh
To these kind efforts made a low reply.

CXIV

Then was the cordial pour'd, and mantle flung
   Around his scarce-clad limbs; and the fair arm
Raised higher the faint head which o'er it hung;
   And her transparent cheek, all pure and warm,
Pillow'd his death-like forehead; then she wrung
   His dewy curls, long drench'd by every storm;
And watch'd with eagerness each throb that drew
A sigh from his heaved bosom—and hers, too.

CXV

And lifting him with care into the cave,
    The gentle girl, and her attendant—one
Young, yet her elder, and of brow less grave,
    And more robust of figure—then begun
To kindle fire, and as the new flames gave
    Light to the rocks that roof'd them, which the sun
Had never seen, the maid, or whatsoe'er
She was, appear'd distinct, and tall, and fair.

CXVI

Her brow was overhung with coins of gold,
    That sparkled o'er the auburn of her hair,
Her clustering hair, whose longer locks were roll'd
    In braids behind; and though her stature were
Even of the highest for a female mould,
    They nearly reach'd her heel; and in her air
There was a something which bespoke command,
As one who was a lady in the land.

CXVII

Her hair, I said, was auburn; but her eyes
    Were black as death, their lashes the same hue,
Of downcast length, in whose silk shadow lies
    Deepest attraction; for when to the view
Forth from its raven fringe the full glance flies,
    Ne'er with such force the swiftest arrow flew;
'Tis as the snake late coil'd, who pours his length,
And hurls at once his venom and his strength.

CXVIII

Her brow was white and low, her cheek's pure dye
    Like twilight rosy still with the set sun;
Short upper lip—sweet lips! that make us sigh
    Ever to have seen such; for she was one

Fit for the model of a statuary
    (A race of mere impostors, when all's done—
I've seen much finer women, ripe and real,
Than all the nonsense of their stone ideal).

CXIX

I'll tell you why I say so, for 'tis just
    One should not rail without a decent cause:
There was an Irish lady, to whose bust
    I ne'er saw justice done, and yet she was
A frequent model; and if e'er she must
    Yield to stern Time and Nature's wrinkling laws,
They will destroy a face which mortal thought
Ne'er compass'd, nor less mortal chisel wrought.

CXX

And such was she, the lady of the cave:
    Her dress was very different from the Spanish,
Simpler, and yet of colours not so grave;
    For, as you know, the Spanish women banish
Bright hues when out of doors, and yet, while wave
    Around them (what I hope will never vanish)
The basquina and the mantilla, they
Seem at the same time mystical and gay.

CXXI

But with our damsel this was not the case:
    Her dress was many-colour'd, finely spun;
Her locks curl'd negligently round her face,
    But through them gold and gems profusely shone;
Her girdle sparkled, and the richest lace
    Flow'd in her veil, and many a precious stone
Flash'd on her little hand; but, what was shocking,
Her small snow feet had slippers, but no stocking.

CXXII

The other female's dress was not unlike,
　　But of inferior materials: she
Had not so many ornaments to strike,
　　Her hair had silver only, bound to be
Her dowry; and her veil, in form alike,
　　Was coarser; and her air, though firm, less free;
Her hair was thicker, but less long; her eyes
As black, but quicker, and of smaller size.

CXXIII

And these two tended him, and cheer'd him both
　　With food and raiment, and those soft attentions,
Which are (as I must own) of female growth,
　　And have ten thousand delicate inventions:
They made a most superior mess of broth,
　　A thing which poesy but seldom mentions,
But the best dish that e'er was cook'd since Homer's
Achilles order'd dinner for new comers.

CXXIV

I'll tell you who they were, this female pair,
　　Lest they should seem princesses in disguise;
Besides, I hate all mystery, and that air
　　Of clap-trap, which your recent poets prize;
And so, in short, the girls they really were
　　They shall appear before your curious eyes,
Mistress and maid; the first was only daughter
Of an old man, who lived upon the water.

CXXV

A fisherman he had been in his youth,
　　And still a sort of fisherman was he;
But other speculations were, in sooth,
　　Added to his connexion with the sea,

Perhaps not so respectable, in truth:
   A little smuggling, and some piracy,
Left him, at last, the sole of many masters
Of an ill-gotten million of piastres.

CXXVI

A fisher, therefore, was he,—though of men,
   Like Peter the Apostle,—and he fish'd
For wandering merchant vessels, now and then,
   And sometimes caught as many as he wish'd;
The cargoes he confiscated, and gain
   He sought in the slave-market too, and dish'd
Full many a morsel for that Turkish trade,
By which, no doubt, a good deal may be made.

CXXVII

He was a Greek, and on his isle had built
   (One of the wild and smaller Cyclades)
A very handsome house from out his guilt,
   And there he lived exceedingly at ease;
Heavens knows what cash he got, or blood he spilt,
   A sad old fellow was he, if you please;
But this I know, it was a spacious building,
Full of barbaric carving, paint, and gilding.

CXXVIII

He had an only daughter, call'd Haidée,
   The greatest heiress of the Eastern Isles;
Besides, so very beautiful was she,
   Her dowry was as nothing to her smiles:
Still in her teens, and like a lovely tree
   She grew to womanhood, and between whiles
Rejected several suitors, just to learn
How to accept a better in his turn.

CXXIX

And walking out upon the beach, below
   The cliff, towards sunset, on that day she found,
Insensible,—not dead, but nearly so,—
   Don Juan, almost famish'd, and half drown'd;
But being naked, she was shock'd, you know,
   Yet deem'd herself in common pity bound,
As far as in her lay, 'to take him in,
A stranger' dying, with so white a skin.

CXXX

But taking him into her father's house
   Was not exactly the best way to save,
But like conveying to the cat the mouse,
   Or people in a trance into their grave;
Because the good old man had so much 'νους',
   Unlike the honest Arab thieves so brave,
He would have hospitably cured the stranger,
And sold him instantly when out of danger.

CXXXI

And therefore, with her maid, she thought it best
   (A virgin always on her maid relies)
To place him in the cave for present rest:
   And when, at last, he open'd his black eyes,
Their charity increased about their guest;
   And their compassion grew to such a size,
It open'd half the turnpike gates to heaven—
(St. Paul says, 'tis the toll which must be given).

CXXXII

They made a fire, but such a fire as they
   Upon the moment could contrive with such
Materials as were cast up round the bay,
   Some broken planks, and oars, that to the touch

Were nearly tinder, since so long they lay
   A mast was almost crumbled to a crutch;
But, by God's grace, here wrecks were in such plenty,
That there was fuel to have furnish'd twenty.

CXXXIII

He had a bed of furs, and a pelisse,
   For Haidée stripp'd her sables off to make
His couch; and, that he might be more at ease,
   And warm, in case by chance he should awake,
They also gave a petticoat apiece,
   She and her maid, and promised by daybreak
To pay him a fresh visit, with a dish
For breakfast, of eggs, coffee, bread, and fish.

CXXXIV

And thus they left him to his lone repose:
   Juan slept like a top, or like the dead,
Who sleep at last, perhaps (God only knows),
   Just for the present; and in his lull'd head
Not even a vision of his former woes
   Throbb'd in accursed dreams, which sometimes spread
Unwelcome visions of our former years,
Till the eye, cheated, opens thick with tears.

CXXXV

Young Juan slept all dreamless:—but the maid,
   Who smooth'd his pillow, as she left the den
Look'd back upon him, and a moment staid,
   And turn'd, believing that he call'd again.
He slumber'd; yet she thought, at least she said
   (The heart will slip, even as the tongue and pen),
He had pronounced her name—but she forgot
That at this moment Juan knew it not.

CXXXVI

And pensive to her father's house she went,
    Enjoining silence strict to Zoe, who
Better than her knew what, in fact, she meant,
    She being wiser by a year or two:
A year or two's an age when rightly spent,
    And Zoe spent hers, as most women do,
In gaining all that useful sort of knowledge
Which is acquired in Nature's good old college.

CXXXVII

The morn broke, and found Juan slumbering still
    Fast in his cave, and nothing clash'd upon
His rest: the rushing of the neighbouring rill,
    And the young beams of the excluded sun,
Troubled him not, and he might sleep his fill;
    And need he had of slumber yet, for none
Had suffer'd more—his hardships were comparative
To those related in my grand-dad's Narrative.

CXXXVIII

Not so Haidée: she sadly toss'd and tumbled,
    And started from her sleep, and, turning o'er,
Dream'd of a thousand wrecks, o'er which she stumbled,
    And handsome corpses strew'd upon the shore;
And woke her maid so early that she grumbled,
    And call'd her father's old slaves up, who swore
In several oaths—Armenian, Turk, and Greek—
They knew not what to think of such a freak.

CXXXIX

But up she got, and up she made them get,
    With some pretence about the sun, that makes
Sweet skies just when he rises, or is set;
    And 'tis, no doubt, a sight to see when breaks

Bright Phœbus, while the mountains still are wet
    With mist, and every bird with him awakes,
And night is flung off like a mourning suit
Worn for a husband,—or some other brute.

CXL

I say, the sun is a most glorious sight:
    I've seen him rise full oft, indeed of late
I have sat up on purpose all the night,
    Which hastens, as physicians say, one's fate;
And so all ye, who would be in the right
    In health and purse, begin your day to date
From daybreak, and when coffin'd at four-score
Engrave upon the plate, you rose at four.

CXLI

And Haidée met the morning face to face;
    Her own was freshest, though a feverish flush
Had dyed it with the headlong blood, whose race
    From heart to cheek is curb'd into a blush,
Like to a torrent which a mountain's base,
    That overpowers some Alpine river's rush,
Checks to a lake, whose waves in circles spread;
Or the Red Sea—but the sea is not red.

CXLII

And down the cliff the island virgin came,
    And near the cave her quick light footsteps drew,
While the sun smiled on her with his first flame,
    And young Aurora kiss'd her lips with dew,
Taking her for a sister; just the same
    Mistake you would have made on seeing the two,
Although the mortal, quite as fresh and fair,
Had all the advantage, too, of not being air.

CXLIII

And when into the cavern Haidée stepp'd
   All timidly, yet rapidly, she saw
That like an infant Juan sweetly slept;
   And then she stopp'd, and stood as if in awe
(For sleep is awful), and on tiptoe crept
   And wrapt him closer, lest the air, too raw,
Should reach his blood, then o'er him still as death
Bent, with hush'd lips, that drank his scarce-drawn breath.

CXLIV

And thus like to an angel o'er the dying
   Who die in righteousness, she lean'd; and there
All tranquilly the shipwreck'd boy was lying,
   As o'er him lay the calm and stirless air:
But Zoe the meantime some eggs was frying,
   Since, after all, no doubt the youthful pair
Must breakfast, and betimes—lest they should ask it,
She drew out her provision from the basket.

CXLV

She knew that the best feelings must have victual,
   And that a shipwreck'd youth would hungry be;
Besides, being less in love, she yawn'd a little,
   And felt her veins chill'd by the neighbouring sea;
And so, she cook'd their breakfast to a tittle;
   I can't say that she gave them any tea,
But there were eggs, fruit, coffee, bread, fish, honey,
With Scio wine,—and all for love, not money.

CXLVI

And Zoe, when the eggs were ready, and
   The coffee made, would fain have waken'd Juan;
But Haidée stopp'd her with her quick small hand,
   And without word, a sign her finger drew on

Her lip, which Zoe needs must understand;
   And, the first breakfast spoilt, prepared a new one,
Because her mistress would not let her break
That sleep which seem'd as it would ne'er awake.

CXLVII

For still he lay, and on his thin worn cheek
   A purple hectic play'd like dying day
On the snow-tops of distant hills; the streak
   Of sufferance yet upon his forehead lay,
Where the blue veins look'd shadowy, shrunk, and weak;
   And his black curls were dewy with the spray,
Which weigh'd upon them yet, all damp and salt,
Mix'd with the stony vapours of the vault.

CXLVIII

And she bent o'er him, and he lay beneath,
   Hush'd as the babe upon its mother's breast,
Droop'd as the willow when no winds can breathe,
   Lull'd like the depth of ocean when at rest,
Fair as the crowning rose of the whole wreath,
   Soft as the callow cygnet in its nest;
In short, he was a very pretty fellow,
Although his woes had turn'd him rather yellow.

CXLIX

He woke and gazed, and would have slept again,
   But the fair face which met his eyes forbade
Those eyes to close, though weariness and pain
   Had further sleep a further pleasure made;
For woman's face was never form'd in vain
   For Juan, so that even when he pray'd
He turn'd from grisly saints, and martyrs hairy,
To the sweet portraits of the Virgin Mary.

CL

And thus upon his elbow he arose,
    And look'd upon the lady, in whose cheek
The pale contended with the purple rose,
    As with an effort she began to speak;
Her eyes were eloquent, her words would pose,
    Although she told him, in good modern Greek,
With an Ionian accent, low and sweet,
That he was faint, and must not talk, but eat.

CLI

Now Juan could not understand a word,
    Being no Grecian; but he had an ear,
And her voice was the warble of a bird,
    So soft, so sweet, so delicately clear,
That finer, simpler music, ne'er was heard;
    The sort of sound we echo with a tear,
Without knowing why—an overpowering tone,
Whence melody descends as from a throne.

CLII

And Juan gazed as one who is awoke
    By a distant organ, doubting if he be
Not yet a dreamer, till the spell is broke
    By the watchman, or some such reality,
Or by one's early valet's cursed knock;
    At least it is a heavy sound to me,
Who like a morning slumber—for the night
Shows stars and women in a better light.

CLIII

And Juan, too, was help'd out from his dream,
    Or sleep, or whatso'er it was, by feeling
A most prodigious appetite; the steam
    Of Zoe's cookery no doubt was stealing

Upon his senses, and the kindling beam
    Of the new fire, which Zoe kept up, kneeling,
To stir her viands, made him quite awake
And long for food, but chiefly a beef-steak. . . .

*   *   *

CLXVII

Return we to Don Juan. He begun
    To hear new words, and to repeat them; but
Some feelings, universal as the sun,
    Where such as could not in his breast be shut
More than within the bosom of a nun:
    He was in love,—as you would be, no doubt,
With a young benefactress,—so was she,
Just in the way we very often see.

CLXVIII

And every day by daybreak—rather early
    For Juan, who was somewhat fond of rest—
She came into the cave, but it was merely
    To see her bird reposing in his nest;
And she would softly stir his locks so curly,
    Without disturbing her yet slumbering guest,
Breathing all gently o'er his cheek and mouth,
As o'er a bed of roses the sweet south.

CLXIX

And every morn his colour freshlier came,
    And every day help'd on his convalescence;
'Twas well, because health in the human frame
    Is pleasant, besides being true love's essence.
For health and idleness to passion's flame
    Are oil and gunpowder; and some good lessons
Are also learnt from Ceres and from Bacchus,
Without whom Venus will not long attack us.

I

CLXX

While Venus fills the heart (without heart really
  Love, though good always, is not quite so good),
Ceres presents a plate of vermicelli,—
  For love must be sustain'd like flesh and blood,
While Bacchus pours out wine, or hands a jelly:
  Eggs, oysters, too, are amatory food;
But who is their purveyor from above
Heaven knows,—it may be Neptune, Pan, or Jove.

CLXXI

When Juan woke he found some good things ready,
  A bath, a breakfast, and the finest eyes
That ever made a youthful heart less steady,
  Besides her maid's, as pretty for their size;
But I have spoken of all this already—
  And repetition's tiresome and unwise,—
Well—Juan, after bathing in the sea,
Came always back to coffee and Haidée.

CLXXII

Both were so young, and one so innocent,
  That bathing pass'd for nothing; Juan seem'd
To her, as 'twere, the kind of being sent,
  Of whom these two years she had nightly dream'd,
A something to be loved, a creature meant
  To be her happiness, and whom she deem'd
To render happy: all who joy would win
Must share it,—Happiness was born a twin.

CLXXIII

It was such pleasure to behold him, such
  Enlargement of existence to partake
Nature with him, to thrill beneath his touch,
  To watch him slumbering, and to see him wake;

To live with him for ever were too much;
    But then the thought of parting made her quake:
He was her own, her ocean-treasure, cast
Like a rich wreck—her first love, and her last.

CLXXIV

And thus a moon roll'd on, and fair Haidée
    Paid daily visits to her boy, and took
Such plentiful precautions, that still he
    Remain'd unknown within his craggy nook;
At last her father's prows put out to sea,
    For certain merchantmen upon the look,
Not as of yore to carry off an Io,
But three Ragusan vessels bound for Scio.

CLXXV

Then came her freedom, for she had no mother,
    So that, her father being at sea, she was
Free as a married woman, or such other
    Female, as where she likes may freely pass,
Without even the encumbrance of a brother,
    The freest she that ever gazed on glass;
I speak of Christian lands in this comparison,
Where wives, at least, are seldom kept in garrison.

CLXXVI

Now she prolong'd her visits and her talk
    (For they must talk), and he had learnt to say
So much as to propose to take a walk,—
    For little had he wander'd since the day
On which, like a young flower snapp'd from the stalk,
    Drooping and dewy on the beach he lay,—
And thus they walk'd out in the afternoon,
And saw the sun set opposite the moon.

CLXXVII

It was a wild and breaker-beaten coast,
  With cliffs above, and a broad sandy shore,
Guarded by shoals and rocks as by an host,
  With here and there a creek, whose aspect wore
A better welcome to the tempest-tost;
  And rarely ceased the haughty billow's roar,
Save on the dead long summer days, which make
The outstretch'd ocean glitter like a lake.

CLXXVIII

And the small ripple spilt upon the beach
  Scarcely o'erpass'd the cream of your champagne,
When o'er the brim the sparkling bumpers reach,
  That spring-dew of the spirit! the heart's rain!
Few things surpass old wine; and they may preach
  Who please,—the more because they preach in vain,—
Let us have wine and women, mirth and laughter,
Sermons and soda-water the day after. . . .

*   *   *

CLXXXI

The coast—I think it was the coast that I
  Was just describing—Yes, it *was* the coast—
Lay at this period quiet as the sky,
  The sands untumbled, the blue waves untost,
And all was stillness, save the sea-bird's cry,
  And dolphin's leap, and little billow crost
By some low rock or shelve, that made it fret
Against the boundary it scarcely wet.

CLXXXII

And forth they wander'd, her sire being gone,
  As I have said, upon an expedition;
And mother, brother, guardian, she had none,
  Save Zoe, who, although with due precision

She waited on her lady with the sun,
  Thought daily service was her only mission,
Bringing warm water, wreathing her long tresses,
And asking now and then for cast-off dresses.

CLXXXIII

It was the cooling hour, just when the rounded
  Red sun sinks down behind the azure hill,
Which then seems as if the whole earth it bounded,
  Circling all nature, hush'd, and dim, and still,
With the far mountain-crescent half surrounded
  On one side, and the deep sea calm and chill,
Upon the other, and the rosy sky,
With one star sparkling through it like an eye.

CLXXXIV

And thus they wander'd forth, and hand in hand,
  Over the shining pebbles and the shells,
Glided along the smooth and harden'd sand,
  And in the worn and wild receptacles
Work'd by the storms, yet work'd as it were plann'd,
  In hollow halls, with sparry roofs and cells,
They turn'd to rest; and, each clasp'd by an arm,
Yielded to the deep twilight's purple charm.

CLXXXV

They look'd up to the sky, whose floating glow
  Spread like a rosy ocean, vast and bright;
They gazed upon the glittering sea below,
  Whence the broad moon rose circling into sight;
They heard the waves splash, and the wind so low,
  And saw each other's dark eyes darting light
Into each other—and, beholding this,
Their lips drew near, and clung into a kiss;

CLXXXVI

A long, long kiss, a kiss of youth, and love,
   And beauty, all concentrating like rays
Into one focus, kindled from above;
   Such kisses as belong to early days,
Where heart, and soul, and sense, in concert move,
   And the blood's lava, and the pulse a blaze,
Each kiss a heart-quake,—for a kiss's strength,
I think it must be reckon'd by its length.

CLXXXVII

By length I mean duration; theirs endured
   Heaven knows how long—no doubt they never reckon'd;
And if they had, they could not have secured
   The sum of their sensations to a second:
They had not spoken; but they felt allured,
   As if their souls and lips each other beckon'd,
Which, being join'd, like swarming bees they clung—
Their hearts the flowers from whence the honey sprung.

CLXXXVIII

They were alone, but not alone as they
   Who shut in chambers think it loneliness;
The silent ocean, and the starlight bay,
   The twilight glow, which momently grew less,
The voiceless sands, and dropping caves, that lay
   Around them, made them to each other press,
As if there were no life beneath the sky
Save theirs, and that their life could never die.

CLXXXIX

They fear'd no eyes nor ears on that lone beach,
   They felt no terrors from the night; they were
All in all to each other; though their speech
   Was broken words, they *thought* a language there,—

And all the burning tongues the passions teach
　　Found in one sigh the best interpreter
Of nature's oracle—first love,—that all
Which Eve has left her daughters since her fall.

CXC

Haidée spoke not of scruples, ask'd no vows,
　　Nor offer'd any; she had never heard
Of plight and promises to be a spouse,
　　Or perils by a loving maid incurr'd;
She was all which pure ignorance allows,
　　And flew to her young mate like a young bird,
And never having dreamt of falsehood, she
Had not one word to say of constancy.

CXCI

She loved, and was beloved—she adored,
　　And she was worshipp'd; after nature's fashion,
Their intense souls, into each other pour'd,
　　If souls could die, had perish'd in that passion,—
But by degrees their senses were restored,
　　Again to be o'ercome, again to dash on;
And, beating 'gainst *his* bosom, Haidée's heart
Felt as if never more to beat apart.

CXCII

Alas! they were so young, so beautiful,
　　So lonely, loving, helpless, and the hour
Was that in which the heart is always full,
　　And, having o'er itself no further power,
Prompts deeds eternity cannot annul,
　　But pays off moments in an endless shower
Of hell-fire—all prepared for people giving
Pleasure or pain to one another living.

CXCIII

Alas! for Juan and Haidée! they were
　So loving and so lovely—till then never,
Excepting our first parents, such a pair
　Had run the risk of being damn'd for ever;
And Haidée, being devout as well as fair,
　Had, doubtless, heard about the Stygian river,
And hell and purgatory—but forgot
Just in the very crisis she should not.

CXCIV

They look upon each other, and their eyes
　Gleam in the moonlight; and her white arm clasps
Round Juan's head, and his around her lies
　Half buried in the tresses which it grasps;
She sits upon his knee, and drinks his sighs,
　He hers, until they end in broken gasps;
And thus they form a group that's quite antique,
Half naked, loving, natural, and Greek.

CXCV

And when those deep and burning moments pass'd,
　And Juan sunk to sleep within her arms,
She slept not, but all tenderly, though fast,
　Sustain'd his head upon her bosom's charms;
And now and then her eye to heaven is cast,
　And then on the pale cheek her breast now warms,
Pillow'd on her o'erflowing heart, which pants
With all it granted, and with all it grants. . . .

* * *

CCII

Haidée was Nature's bride, and knew not this;
　Haidée was Passion's child, born where the sun
Showers triple light, and scorches even the kiss
　Of his gazelle-eyed daughters; she was one

Made but to love, to feel that she was his
    Who was her chosen: what was said or done
Elsewhere was nothing.—She had nought to fear,
Hope, care, nor love beyond,—her heart beat *here*.

CCIII

And oh! that quickening of the heart, that beat!
    How much it costs us! yet each rising throb
Is in its cause as its effect so sweet,
    That Wisdom, ever on the watch to rob
Joy of its alchymy, and to repeat
    Fine truths; even Conscience, too, has a tough job
To make us understand each good old maxim,
So good—I wonder Castlereagh don't tax 'em.

CCIV

And now 'twas done—on the lone shore were plighted
    Their hearts; the stars, their nuptial torches, shed
Beauty upon the beautiful they lighted:
    Ocean their witness, and the cave their bed,
By their own feelings hallow'd and united,
    Their priest was Solitude, and they were wed:
And they were happy, for to their young eyes
Each was an angel, and earth paradise. . . .

CANTO III

I

Hail, Muse! *et cætera.*—We left Juan sleeping,
   Pillow'd upon a fair and happy breast,
And watch'd by eyes that never yet knew weeping,
   And loved by a young heart, too deeply blest
To feel the poison through her spirit creeping,
   Or know who rested there, a foe to rest,
Had soil'd the current of her sinless years,
And turn'd her pure heart's purest blood to tears.

II

Oh, Love! what is it in this world of ours
   Which makes it fatal to be loved? Ah why
With cypress branches hast thou wreathed thy bowers,
   And made thy best interpreter a sigh?
As those who dote on odours pluck the flowers,
   And place them on their breast—but place to die—
Thus the frail beings we would fondly cherish
Are laid within our bosoms but to perish.

III

In her first passion woman loves her lover,
   In all the others all she loves is love,
Which grows a habit she can ne'er get over,
   And fits her loosely—like an easy glove,
As you may find, whene'er you like to prove her:
   One man alone at first her heart can move;
She then prefers him in the plural number,
Not finding that the additions much encumber.

IV

I know not if the fault be men's or theirs;
    But one thing's pretty sure; a woman planted—
(Unless at once she plunge for life in prayers)—
    After a decent time must be gallanted;
Although, no doubt, her first of love affairs
    Is that to which her heart is wholly granted;
Yet there are some, they say, who have had *none*,
But those who have ne'er end with only *one*.

V

'Tis melancholy, and a fearful sign
    Of human frailty, folly, also crime,
That love and marriage rarely can combine,
    Although they both are born in the same clime;
Marriage from love, like vinegar from wine—
    A sad, sour, sober beverage—by time
Is sharpen'd from its high celestial flavour
Down to a very homely household savour.

VI

There's something of antipathy, as 't were,
    Between their present and their future state;
A kind of flattery that's hardly fair
    Is used until the truth arrives too late—
Yet what can people do, except despair?
    The same things change their names at such a rate;
For instance—passion in a lover's glorious,
But in a husband is pronounced uxorious. . . .

*   *   *

XII

Haidée and Juan were not married, but
    The fault was theirs, not mine: it is not fair,
Chaste reader, then, in any way to put
    The blame on me, unless you wish they were;

Then if you'd have them wedded, please to shut
　　The book which treats of this erroneous pair,
Before the consequences grow too awful;
　'Tis dangerous to read of loves unlawful.

XIII

Yet they were happy,—happy in the illicit
　　Indulgence of their innocent desires;
But more imprudent grown with every visit,
　　Haidée forgot the island was her sire's:
When we have what we like, 'tis hard to miss it,
　　At least in the beginning, ere one tires;
Thus she came often, not a moment losing,
Whilst her piratical papa was cruising.

XIV

Let not his mode of raising cash seem strange,
　　Although he fleeced the flags of every nation,
For into a prime minister but change
　　His title, and 'tis nothing but taxation;
But he, more modest, took an humbler range
　　Of life, and in an honester vocation
Pursued o'er the high seas his watery journey,
And merely practised as a sea-attorney.

XV

The good old gentleman had been detain'd
　　By winds and waves, and some important captures;
And, in the hope of more, at sea remain'd,
　　Although a squall or two had damp'd his raptures,
By swamping one of the prizes; he had chain'd
　　His prisoners, dividing them like chapters
In number'd lots; they all had cuffs and collars,
And averaged each from ten to a hundred dollars.

XVI

Some he disposed of off Cape Matapan,
  Among his friends the Mainots; some he sold,
To his Tunis correspondents, save one man
  Toss'd overboard unsaleable (being old);
The rest—save here and there some richer one,
  Reserved for future ransom in the hold—
Were link'd alike, as for the common people he
Had a large order from the Dey of Tripoli.

XVII

The merchandise was served in the same way,
  Pieced out for different marts in the Levant,
Except some certain portions of the prey,
  Light classic articles of female want,
French stuffs, lace, tweezers, toothpicks, teapot, tray,
  Guitars and castanets from Alicant,
All which selected from the spoils he gathers,
Robb'd for his daughter by the best of fathers.

XVIII

A monkey, a Dutch mastiff, a mackaw,
  Two parrots, with a Persian cat and kittens,
He chose from several animals he saw—
  A terrier, too, which once had been a Briton's,
Who dying on the coast of Ithaca,
  The peasants gave the poor dumb thing a pittance;
These to secure in this strong blowing weather,
He caged in one huge hamper all together.

XIX

Then having settled his marine affairs,
  Despatching single cruisers here and there,
His vessel having need of some repairs,
  He shaped his course to where his daughter fair

Continued still her hospitable cares;
　But that part of the coast being shoal and bare,
And rough with reefs which ran out many a mile,
His port lay on the other side o' the isle.

XX

And there he went ashore without delay,
　Having no custom-house nor quarantine
To ask him awkward questions on the way
　About the time and place where he had been:
He left his ship to be hove down next day,
　With orders to the people to careen;
So that all hands were busy beyond measure,
In getting out goods, ballast, guns, and treasure.

XXI

Arriving at the summit of a hill
　Which overlook'd the white walls of his home,
He stopp'd.—What singular emotions fill
　Their bosoms who have been induced to roam!
With fluttering doubts if all be well or ill—
　With love for many, and with fears for some;
All feelings which o'erleap the years long lost,
And bring our hearts back to their starting-post. . . .

＊　　＊　　＊

XXVII

He saw his white walls shining in the sun,
　His garden trees all shadowy and green;
He heard his rivulet's light bubbling run,
　The distant dog-bark; and perceived between
The umbrage of the wood so cool and dun,
　The moving figures, and the sparkling sheen
Of arms (in the East all arm)—and various dyes
Of colour'd garbs, as bright as butterflies.

XXVIII

And as the spot where they appear he nears,
   Surprised at these unwonted signs of idling,
He hears—alas! no music of the spheres,
   But an unhallow'd, earthly sound of fiddling!
A melody which made him doubt his ears,
   The cause being past his guessing or unriddling;
A pipe, too, and a drum, and shortly after,
A most unoriental roar of laughter.

XXIX

And still more nearly to the place advancing,
   Descending rather quickly the declivity,
Through the waved branches, o'er the greensward
    glancing,
   'Midst other indications of festivity,
Seeing a troop of his domestics dancing
   Like dervises, who turn as on a pivot, he
Perceived it was the Pyrrhic dance so martial,
To which the Levantines are very partial.

XXX

And further on a group of Grecian girls,
   The first and tallest her white kerchief waving,
Were strung together like a row of pearls,
   Link'd hand in hand, and dancing; each too having
Down her white neck long floating auburn curls—
   (The least of which would set ten poets raving);
Their leader sang—and bounded to her song,
With choral step and voice, the virgin throng.

XXXI

And here, assembled cross-legg'd round their trays,
   Small social parties just begun to dine;
Pilaus and meats of all sorts met the gaze,
   And flasks of Samian and of Chian wine,

And sherbet cooling in the porous vase;
   Above them their dessert grew on its vine,
The orange and pomegranate nodding o'er
Dropp'd in their laps, scarce pluck'd, their mellow store.

XXXII

A band of children, round a snow-white ram,
   There wreathe his venerable horns with flowers;
While peaceful as if still an unwean'd lamb,
   The patriarch of the flock all gently cowers
His sober head, majestically tame,
   Or eats from out the palm, or playful lowers,
His brow, as if in act to butt, and then
Yielding to their small hands, draws back again.

XXXIII

Their classical profiles, and glittering dresses,
   Their large black eyes, and soft seraphic cheeks,
Crimson as cleft pomegranates, their long tresses,
   The gesture which enchants, the eye that speaks,
The innocence which happy childhood blesses,
   Made quite a picture of these little Greeks;
So that the philosophical beholder
Sigh'd for their sakes—that they should e'er grow older.

XXXIV

Afar, a dwarf buffoon stood telling tales,
   To a sedate grey circle of old smokers,
Of secret treasures found in hidden vales,
   Of wonderful replies from Arab jokers,
Of charms to make good gold and cure bad ails,
   Of rocks bewitch'd that open to the knockers,
Of magic ladies who, by one sole act,
Transform'd their lords to beasts (but that's a fact).

XXXV

Here was no lack of innocent diversion
   For the imagination or the senses,
Song, dance, wine, music, stories from the Persian,
   All pretty pastimes in which no offence is;
But Lambro saw all these things with aversion,
   Perceiving in his absence such expenses,
Dreading that climax of all human ills,
The inflammation of his weekly bills.

XXXVI

Ah! what is man? what perils still environ
   The happiest mortals even after dinner?
A day of gold from out an age of iron
   Is all that life allows the luckiest sinner;
Pleasure (whene'er she sings, at least) 's a siren,
   That lures, to flay alive, the young beginner;
Lambro's reception at his people's banquet
Was such as fire accords to a wet blanket.

XXXVII

He—being a man who seldom used a word
   Too much, and wishing gladly to surprise
(In general he surprised men with the sword)
   His daughter—had not sent before to advise
Of his arrival, so that no one stirr'd;
   And long he paused to reassure his eyes,
In fact much more astonish'd than delighted,
To find so much good company invited.

XXXVIII

He did not know (alas! how men will lie!)
   That a report (especially the Greeks)
Avouch'd his death (such people never die),
   And put his house in mourning several weeks,—

K

But now their eyes and also lips were dry;
   The bloom too had return'd to Haidée's cheeks.
Her tears too being return'd into their fount,
She now kept house upon her own account.

XXXIX

Hence all this rice, meat, dancing, wine, and fiddling,
   Which turn'd the isle into a place of pleasure;
The servants all were getting drunk or idling,
   A life which made them happy beyond measure.
Her father's hospitality seem'd middling,
   Compared with what Haidée did with his treasure;
'Twas wonderful how things went on improving,
While she had not one hour to spare from loving.

XL

Perhaps you think, in stumbling on this feast,
   He flew into a passion, and in fact
There was no mighty reason to be pleased;
   Perhaps you prophesy some sudden act,
The whip, the rack, or dungeon at the least,
   To teach his people to be more exact,
And that, proceeding at a very high rate,
He show'd the royal *penchants* of a pirate.

XLI

You're wrong.—He was the mildest manner'd man
   That ever scuttled ship or cut a throat,
With such true breeding of a gentleman,
   You never could divine his real thought;
No courtier could, and scarcely woman can
   Gird more deceit within a petticoat;
Pity he loved adventurous life's variety,
He was so great a loss to good society. . . .

*   *   *

LII

He enter'd in the house—his home no more,
  For without hearts there is no home;—and felt
The solitude of passing his own door
  Without a welcome: *there* he long had dwelt,
There his few peaceful days Time had swept o'er,
  There his warm bosom and keen eye would melt
Over the innocence of that sweet child,
His only shrine of feelings undefiled.

LIII

He was a man of a strange temperament,
  Of mild demeanour though of savage mood,
Moderate in all his habits, and content
  With temperance in pleasure, as in food,
Quick to perceive, and strong to bear, and meant
  For something better, if not wholly good;
His country's wrongs and his despair to save her
Had stung him from a slave to an enslaver.

LIV

The love of power, and rapid gain of gold,
  The hardness by long habitude produced,
The dangerous life in which he had grown old,
  The mercy he had granted oft abused,
The sights he was accustom'd to behold,
  The wild seas, and wild men with whom he cruised,
Had cost his enemies a long repentance,
And made him a good friend, but bad acquaintance.

LV

But something of the spirit of old Greece
  Flash'd o'er his soul a few heroic rays,
Such as lit onward to the Golden Fleece
  His predecessors in the Colchian days;

'Tis true he had no ardent love for peace—
   Alas! his country show'd no path to praise:
Hate to the world and war with every nation
He waged, in vengeance of her degradation.

LVI

Still o'er his mind the influence of the clime
   Shed its Ionian elegance, which show'd
Its power unconsciously full many a time,—
   A taste seen in the choice of his abode,
A love of music and of scenes sublime,
   A pleasure in the gentle stream that flow'd
Past him in crystal, and a joy in flowers,
Bedew'd his spirit in his calmer hours.

LVII

But whatsoe'er he had of love reposed
   On that beloved daughter: she had been
The only thing which kept his heart unclosed
   Amidst the savage deeds he had done and seen,
A lonely pure affection unopposed:
   There wanted but the loss of this to wean
His feelings from all milk of human kindness,
And turn him like the Cyclops mad with blindness. . . .

*   *   *

LXI

Old Lambro pass'd unseen a private gate,
   And stood within his hall at eventide;
Meantime the lady and her lover sate
   At wassail in their beauty and their pride:
An ivory inlaid table spread with state
   Before them, and fair slaves on every side;
Gems, gold, and silver, form'd the service mostly,
Mother of pearl and coral the less costly.

LXII

The dinner made about a hundred dishes;
  Lamb and pistachio nuts—in short, all meats,
And saffron soups, and sweetbreads; and the fishes
  Were of the finest that e'er flounced in nets,
Drest to a Sybarite's most pamper'd wishes;
  The beverage was various sherbets
Of raisin, orange, and pomegranate juice,
Squeezed through the rind, which makes it best for use.

LXIII

These were ranged round, each in its crystal ewer,
  And fruits and date-bread loaves closed the repast,
And Mocha's berry, from Arabia pure,
  In small fine China cups, came in at last;
Gold cups of filigree made to secure
  The hand from burning underneath them placed,
Cloves, cinnamon, and saffron too were boil'd
Up with the coffee, which (I think) they spoil'd. . . .

*   *   *

LXVII

Haidée and Juan carpeted their feet
  On crimson satin, border'd with pale blue;
Their sofa occupied three parts complete
  Of the apartment—and appear'd quite new;
The velvet cushions (for a throne more meet)
  Were scarlet, from whose glowing centre grew
A sun emboss'd in gold, whose rays of tissue,
Meridian-like, were seen all light to issue.

LXVIII

Crystal and marble, plate and porcelain,
  Had done their work of splendour; Indian mats
And Persian carpets, which the heart bled to stain,
  Over the floors were spread; gazelles and cats,

And dwarfs and blacks, and such like things that gain
    Their bread as ministers and favourites—(that's
To say, by degradation)—mingled there
As plentiful as in a court or fair.

LXIX

There was no want of lofty mirrors, and
    The tables, most of ebony inlaid
With mother of pearl or ivory, stood at hand,
    Or were of tortoise-shell or rare woods made,
Fretted with gold or silver:—by command,
    The greater part of these were ready spread
With viands and sherbets in ice—and wine—
Kept for all comers at all hours to dine.

LXX

Of all the dresses I select Haidée's:
    She wore two jelicks—one was of pale yellow;
Of azure, pink, and white was her chemise—
    'Neath which her breast heaved like a little billow;
With buttons form'd of pearls as large as peas,
    All gold and crimson shone her jelick's fellow,
And the striped white gauze baracan that bound her,
Like fleecy clouds about the moon, flow'd round her.

LXXI

One large gold bracelet clasp'd each lovely arm,
    Lockless—so pliable from the pure gold
That the hand stretch'd and shut it without harm,
    The limb which it adorn'd its only mould;
So beautiful—its very shape would charm,
    And clinging as if loth to lose its hold,
The purest ore enclosed the whitest skin
That e'er by precious metal was held in.

LXXII

Around, as princess of her father's land,
   A like gold bar above her instep roll'd
Announced her rank; twelve rings were on her hand;
   Her hair was starr'd with gems; her veil's fine fold
Below her breast was fasten'd with a band
   Of lavish pearls, whose worth could scarce be told;
Her orange silk full Turkish trousers furl'd
About the prettiest ankle in the world.

LXXIII

Her hair's long auburn waves down to her heel
   Flow'd like an Alpine torrent which the sun
Dyes with his morning light,—and would conceal
   Her person if allow'd at large to run,
And still they seem'd resentfully to feel
   The silken fillet's curb, and sought to shun
Their bonds whene'er some Zephyr caught began
To offer his young pinion as her fan.

LXXIV

Round her she made an atmosphere of life,
   The very air seem'd lighter from her eyes,
They were so soft and beautiful, and rife
   With all we can imagine of the skies,
And pure as Psyche ere she grew a wife—
   Too pure even for the purest human ties;
Her overpowering presence made you feel
It would not be idolatry to kneel.

LXXV

Her eyelashes, though dark as night, were tinged
   (It is the country's custom), but in vain;
For those large black eyes were so blackly fringed,
   The glossy rebels mock'd the jetty stain,

And in their native beauty stood avenged:
   Her nails were touch'd with henna; but again
The power of art was turn'd to nothing, for
They could not look more rosy than before.

LXXVI

The henna should be deeply dyed to make
   The skin relieved appear more fairly fair;
She had no need of this, day ne'er will break
   On mountain-tops more heavenly white than her:
The eye might doubt if it were well awake,
   She was so like a vision; I might err,
But Shakespeare also says, 'tis very silly
'To gild refined gold, or paint the lily.'

LXXVII

Juan had on a shawl of black and gold,
   But a white baracan, and so transparent
The sparkling gems beneath you might behold,
   Like small stars through the milky way apparent;
His turban, furl'd in many a graceful fold,
   An emerald aigrette with Haidée's hair in't
Surmounted as its clasp, a glowing crescent,
Whose rays shone ever trembling, but incessant.

LXXVIII

And now they were diverted by their suite,
   Dwarfs, dancing-girls, black eunuchs, and a poet,
Which made their new establishment complete;
   The last was of great fame, and liked to show it;
His verses rarely wanted their due feet—
   And for his theme—he seldom sung below it,
He being paid to satirise or flatter,
As the psalm says, 'inditing a good matter.' . . .

*   *   *

LXXXIV

He had travell'd 'mongst the Arabs, Turks, and Franks,
    And knew the self-loves of the different nations;
And having lived with people of all ranks,
    Had something ready upon most occasions—
Which got him a few presents and some thanks.
    He varied with some skill his adulations;
To 'do at Rome as Romans do', a piece
Of conduct was which he observed in Greece.

LXXXV

Thus, usually, when he was asked to sing,
    He gave the different nations something national;
'Twas all the same to him—'God save the king',
    Or '*Ça ira*', according to the fashion all:
His muse made increment of any thing,
    From the high lyric down to the low rational:
If Pindar sang horse-races, what should hinder
Himself from being as pliable as Pindar?

LXXXVI

In France, for instance, he would write a chanson;
    In England a six canto quarto tale;
In Spain he'd make a ballad or romance on
    The last war—much the same in Portugal;
In Germany, the Pegasus he'd prance on
    Would be old Goethe's—(see what says De Staël);
In Italy he'd ape the 'Trecentisti';
In Greece, he'd sing some sort of hymn like this t'ye:

1

The isles of Greece, the isles of Greece!
    Where burning Sappho loved and sung,
Where grew the arts of war and peace,
    Where Delos rose, and Phœbus sprung!
Eternal summer gilds them yet,
But all, except their sun, is set.

2

The Scian and the Teian muse,
    The hero's harp, the lover's lute,
Have found the fame your shores refuse
    Their place of birth alone is mute
To sounds which echo further west
Than your sires' 'Islands of the Blest'.

3

The mountains look on Marathon—
    And Marathon looks on the sea;
And musing there an hour alone,
    I dream'd that Greece might still be free;
For standing on the Persians' grave,
I could not deem myself a slave.

4

A king sate on the rocky brow
    Which looks o'er sea-born Salamis;
And ships, by thousands, lay below,
    And men in nations;—all were his!
He counted them at break of day—
And when the sun set where were they?

5

And where are they? and where art thou,
    My country? On thy voiceless shore
The heroic lay is tuneless now—
    The heroic bosom beats no more!
And must thy lyre, so long divine,
Degenerate into hands like mine?

6

'Tis something, in the dearth of fame,
　　Though link'd among a fetter'd race,
To feel at least a patriot's shame,
　　Even as I sing, suffuse my face;
For what is left the poet here?
For Greeks a blush—for Greece a tear.

7

Must *we* but weep o'er days more blest?
　　Must *we* but blush?—Our fathers bled.
Earth! render back from out thy breast
　　A remnant of our Spartan dead!
Of the three hundred grant but three,
To make a new Thermopylæ!

8

What, silent still? and silent all?
　　Ah! no;—the voices of the dead
Sound like a distant torrent's fall,
　　And answer, 'Let one living head,
But one arise,—we come, we come!'
'Tis but the living who are dumb.

9

In vain—in vain: strike other chords;
　　Fill high the cup with Samian wine!
Leave battles to the Turkish hordes,
　　And shed the blood of Scio's vine!
Hark! rising to the ignoble call—
How answers each bold bacchanal!

10

You have the Pyrrhic dance as yet;
    Where is the Pyrrhic phalanx gone?
Of two such lessons, why forget
    The nobler and the manlier one?
You have the letters Cadmus gave—
Think ye he meant them for a slave?

11

Fill high the bowl with Samian wine!
    We will not think of themes like these!
It made Anacreon's song divine:
    He served—but served Polycrates—
A tyrant; but our masters then
Were still, at least, our countrymen.

12

The tyrant of the Chersonese
    Was freedom's best and bravest friend;
That tyrant was Miltiades!
    Oh, that the present hour would lend
Another despot of the kind!
Such chains as his were sure to bind.

13

Fill high the bowl with Samian wine!
    On Suli's rock, and Parga's shore,
Exists the remnant of a line
    Such as the Doric mothers bore;
And there, perhaps, some seed is sown,
The Heracleidan blood might own.

14

Trust not for freedom to the Franks—
  They have a king who buys and sells;
In native swords, and native ranks,
  The only hope of courage dwells;
But Turkish force, and Latin fraud,
Would break your shield, however broad.

15

Fill high the bowl with Samian wine!
  Our virgins dance beneath the shade—
I see their glorious black eyes shine;
  But gazing on each glowing maid,
My own the burning tear-drop laves,
To think such breasts must suckle slaves.

16

Place me on Sunium's marbled steep,
  Where nothing, save the waves and I,
May hear our mutual murmurs sweep;
  There, swan-like, let me sing and die:
A land of slaves shall ne'er be mine—
Dash down yon cup of Samian wine!

LXXXVII

Thus sung, or would, or could, or should have sung,
  The modern Greek, in tolerable verse;
If not like Orpheus quite, when Greece was young,
  Yet in these times he might have done much worse:
His strain display'd some feeling—right or wrong;
  And feeling, in a poet, is the source
Of others' feeling; but they are such liars,
And take all colours—like the hands of dyers.

LXXXVIII

But words are things, and a small drop of ink,
 Falling like dew, upon a thought, produces
That which makes thousands, perhaps millions, think
 'Tis strange, the shortest letter which man uses
Instead of speech, may form a lasting link
 Of ages; to what straits old Time reduces
Frail man, when paper—even a rag like this,
Survives himself, his tomb, and all that's his!

LXXXIX

And when his bones are dust, his grave a blank,
 His station, generation, even his nation,
Become a thing, or nothing, save to rank
 In chronological commemoration,
Some dull MS. oblivion long has sank,
 Or graven stone found in a barrack's station
In digging the foundation of a closet,
May turn his name up, as a rare deposit.

XC

And glory long has made the sages smile;
 'Tis something, nothing, words, illusion, wind—
Depending more upon the historian's style
 Than on the name a person leaves behind:
Troy owes to Homer what whist owes to Hoyle:
 The present century was growing blind
To the great Marlborough's skill in giving knocks,
Until his late Life by Archdeacon Coxe.

XCI

Milton's the prince of poets—so we say;
 A little heavy, but no less divine:
An independent being in his day—
 Learn'd, pious, temperate in love and wine;

But his life falling into Johnson's way,
  We're told this great high priest of all the Nine
Was whipt at college—a harsh sire—odd spouse,
For the first Mrs. Milton left his house.

XCII

All these are, *certes*, entertaining facts,
  Like Shakespeare's stealing deer, Lord Bacon's bribes;
Like Titus' youth, and Cæsar's earliest acts;
  Like Burns (whom Doctor Currie well describes);
Like Cromwell's pranks;—but although truth exacts
  These amiable descriptions from the scribes,
As most essential to their hero's story,
They do not much contribute to his glory.

XCIII

All are not moralists, like Southey, when
  He prated to the world of 'Pantisocrasy';
Or Wordsworth unexcised, unhired, who then
  Season'd his pedlar poems with democracy;
Or Coleridge, long before his flighty pen
  Let to the Morning Post its aristocracy;
When he and Southey, following the same path,
Espoused two partners (milliners of Bath).

XCIV

Such names at present cut a convict figure,
  The very Botany Bay in moral geography;
Their loyal treason, renegado rigour,
  Are good manure for their more bare biography,
Wordsworth's last quarto, by the way, is bigger
  Than any since the birthday of typography;
A drowsy frowzy poem, call'd the 'Excursion',
Writ in a manner which is my aversion.

XCV

He there builds up a formidable dyke
    Between his own and others' intellect:
But Wordsworth's poem, and his followers, like
    Joanna Southcote's Shiloh, and her sect,
Are things which in this century don't strike
    The public mind,—so few are the elect;
And the new births of both their stale virginities
Have proved but dropsies, taken for divinities.

XCVI

But let me to my story: I must own,
    If I have any fault, it is digression,
Leaving my people to proceed alone,
    While I soliloquize beyond expression;
But these are my addresses from the throne,
    Which put off business to the ensuing session:
Forgetting each omission is a loss to
The world, not quite so great as Ariosto.

XCVII

I know that what our neighbours call *'longueurs'*,
    (We've not so good a *word*, but have the *thing*,
In that complete perfection which insures
    An epic from Bob Southey every Spring—)
Form not the true temptation which allures
    The reader; but 'twould not be hard to bring
Some fine examples of the *epopée*,
To prove its grand ingredient is *ennui*.

XCVIII

We learn from Horace, 'Homer sometimes sleeps';
    We feel without him, Wordsworth sometimes wakes,
To show with what complacency he creeps,
    With his dear *'Waggoners'*, around his lakes.

He wishes for 'a boat' to sail the deeps—
　　Of ocean?—No, of air; and then he makes
Another outcry for 'a little boat',
And drivels seas to set it well afloat.

XCIX

If he must fain sweep o'er the ethereal plain
　　And Pegasus runs restive in his 'waggon',
Could he not beg the loan of Charles's Wain?
　　Or pray Medea for a single dragon?
Or if, too classic for his vulgar brain,
　　He fear'd his neck to venture such a nag on,
And he must needs mount nearer to the moon,
Could not the blockhead ask for a balloon?

C

'Pedlars', and 'boats', and 'waggons'! Oh! ye shades
　　Of Pope and Dryden, are we come to this?
That trash of such sort not alone evades
　　Contempt, but from the bathos' vast abyss
Floats scumlike uppermost, and these Jack Cades
　　Of sense and song above your graves may hiss—
The 'little boatman' and his 'Peter Bell'
Can sneer at him who drew 'Achitophel'!

CI

T'our tale.—The feast was over, the slaves gone,
　　The dwarfs and dancing girls had all retired;
The Arab lore and poet's song were done,
　　And every sound of revelry expired;
The lady and her lover, left alone,
　　The rosy flood of twilight's sky admired;—
Ave Maria! o'er the earth and sea,
That heavenliest hour of Heaven is worthiest thee!
L

CII

Ave Maria! blessed be the hour!
  The time, the clime, the spot, where I so oft
Have felt that moment in its fullest power
  Sink o'er the earth so beautiful and soft,
While swung the deep bell in the distant tower,
  Or the faint dying day-hymn stole aloft,
And not a breath crept through the rosy air,
And yet the forest leaves seem'd stirr'd with prayer.

CIII

Ave Maria! 'tis the hour of prayer!
  Ave Maria! 'tis the hour of love!
Ave Maria! may our spirits dare
  Look up to thine and to thy Son's above!
Ave Maria! oh that face so fair!
  Those downcast eyes beneath the Almighty dove—
What though 'tis but a pictured image strike—
That painting is no idol,—'tis too like.

CIV

Some kinder casuists are pleased to say,
  In nameless print—that I have no devotion;
But set those persons down with me to pray,
  And you shall see who has the properest notion
Of getting into Heaven the shortest way;
  My altars are the mountains and the ocean,
Earth, air, stars,—all that springs from the great Whole,
Who hath produced, and will receive the soul.

CV

Sweet hour of twilight!—in the solitude
  Of the pine forest, and the silent shore
Which bounds Ravenna's immemorial wood,
  Rooted where once the Adrian wave flow'd o'er,

To where the last Cæsarean fortress stood,
  Evergreen forest! which Boccaccio's lore
And Dryden's lay made haunted ground to me,
How have I loved the twilight hour and thee!

CVI

The shrill cicalas, people of the pine,
  Making their summer lives one ceaseless song,
Were the sole echoes, save my steed's and mine,
  And vesper bells' that rose the boughs along;
The spectre huntsman of Onesti's line,
  His hell-dogs, and their chase, and the fair throng
Which learn'd from this example not to fly
From a true lover, shadow'd my mind's eye.

CVII

Oh, Hesperus! thou bringest all good things—
  Home to the weary, to the hungry cheer,
To the young bird the parent's brooding wings,
  The welcome stall to the o'erlabour'd steer;
Whate'er of peace about our hearthstone clings,
  Whate'er our household gods protect of dear,
Are gather'd round us by thy look of rest;
Thou bring'st the child, too, to the mother's breast.

CVIII

Soft hour! which wakes the wish and melts the heart
  Of those who sail the seas, on the first day
When they from their sweet friends are torn apart;
  Or fills with love the pilgrim on his way
As the far bell of vesper makes him start,
  Seeming to weep the dying day's decay;
Is this a fancy which our reason scorns?
Ah! surely nothing dies but something mourns!

CIX

When Nero perish'd by the justest doom
   Which ever the destroyer yet destroy'd,
Amidst the roar of liberated Rome,
   Of nations freed, and the world overjoy'd,
Some hands unseen strew'd flowers upon his tomb
   Perhaps the weakness of a heart not void
Of feeling for some kindness done, when power
Had left the wretch an uncorrupted hour.

CX

But I'm digressing; what on earth has Nero,
   Or any such like sovereign buffoons,
To do with the transactions of my hero,
   More than such madmen's fellow man—the moon's?
Sure my invention must be down at zero,
   And I grown one of many 'wooden spoons'
Of verse (the name with which we Cantabs please
To dub the last of honours in degrees).

CXI

I feel this tediousness will never do—
   'Tis being *too* epic, and I must cut down
(In copying) this long canto into two;
   They'll never find it out, unless I own
The fact, excepting some experienced few;
   And then as an improvement 'twill be shown:
I'll prove that such the opinion of the critic is
From Aristotle *passim*.—See Ποιητικῆς.

CANTO IV

I

Nothing so difficult as a beginning
    In poesy, unless perhaps the end;
For oftentimes when Pegasus seems winning
    The race, he sprains a wing, and down we tend,
Like Lucifer when hurl'd from heaven for sinning;
    Our sin the same, and hard as his to mend,
Being pride, which leads the mind to soar too far,
Till our own weakness shows us what we are.

II

But time, which brings all beings to their level,
    And sharp Adversity, will teach at last
Man,—and, as we would hope,—perhaps the devil,
    That neither of their intellects are vast:
While youth's hot wishes in our red veins revel,
    We know not this—the blood flows on too fast:
But as the torrent widens towards the ocean,
We ponder deeply on each past emotion.

III

As boy, I thought myself a clever fellow,
    And wish'd that others held the same opinion;
They took it up when my days grew more mellow,
    And other minds acknowledged my dominion:
Now my sere fancy 'falls into the yellow
    Leaf', and Imagination droops her pinion,
And the sad truth which hovers o'er my desk
Turns what was once romantic to burlesque.

IV

And if I laugh at any mortal thing,
   'Tis that I may not weep; and if I weep,
'Tis that our nature cannot always bring
   Itself to apathy, for we must steep
Our hearts first in the depths of Lethe's spring,
   Ere what we least wish to behold will sleep:
Thetis baptized her mortal son in Styx;
A mortal mother would on Lethe fix.

V

Some have accused me of a strange design
   Against the creed and morals of the land,
And trace it in this poem every line;
   I don't pretend that I quite understand
My own meaning when I would be *very* fine;
   But the fact is that I have nothing plann'd,
Unless it were to be a moment merry,
A novel word in my vocabulary.

VI

To the kind reader of our sober clime
   This way of writing will appear exotic;
Pulci was sire of the half-serious rhyme,
   Who sang when chivalry was more Quixotic,
And revell'd in the fancies of the time,
   True knights, chaste dames, huge giant kings despotic;
But all these, save the last, being obsolete,
I chose a modern subject as more meet.

VII

How I have treated it, I do not know;
   Perhaps no better than they have treated me,
Who have imputed such designs as show
   Not what they saw, but what they wish'd to see;

But if it gives them pleasure, be it so,
    This is a liberal age, and thoughts are free:
Meantime Apollo plucks me by the ear,
And tells me to resume my story here.

VIII

Young Juan and his lady-love were left
    To their own hearts' most sweet society;
Even Time the pitiless in sorrow cleft
    With his rude scythe such gentle bosoms; he
Sigh'd to behold them of their hours bereft,
    Though foe to love; and yet they could not be
Meant to grow old, but die in happy spring,
Before one charm or hope had taken wing.

IX

Their faces were not made for wrinkles, their
    Pure blood to stagnate, their great hearts to fail;
The blank grey was not made to blast their hair,
    But like the climes that know nor snow nor hail,
They were all summer; lightning might assail
    And shiver them to ashes, but to trail
A long and snake-like life of dull decay
Was not for them—they had too little clay.

X

They were alone once more; for them to be
    Thus was another Eden; they were never
Weary, unless when separate: the tree
    Cut from its forest root of years—the river
Damm'd from its fountain—the child from the knee
    And breast maternal wean'd at once for ever,—
Would wither less than these two torn apart;
Alas! there is no instinct like the heart—

XI

The heart—which may be broken: happy they!
   Thrice fortunate! who of that fragile mould,
The precious porcelain of human clay,
   Break with the first fall: they can ne'er behold
The long year link'd with heavy day on day,
   And all which must be borne, and never told;
While life's strange principle will often lie
Deepest in those who long the most to die.

XII

'Whom the gods love die young' was said of yore,
   And many deaths do they escape by this:
The death of friends, and that which slays even more—
   The death of friendship, love, youth, all that is,
Except mere breath; and since the silent shore
   Awaits at last even those who longest miss
The old archer's shafts, perhaps the early grave
Which men weep over may be meant to save.

XIII

Haidée and Juan thought not of the dead.
   The heavens and earth, and air, seem'd made for them;
They found no fault with Time, save that he fled;
   They saw not in themselves aught to condemn;
Each was the other's mirror, and but read
   Joy sparkling in their dark eyes like a gem,
And knew such brightness was but the reflection
Of their exchanging glances of affection.

XIV

The gentle pressure, and the thrilling touch,
   The least glance better understood than words,
Which still said all, and ne'er could say too much;
   A language, too, but like to that of birds,

Known but to them, at least appearing such
   As but to lovers a true sense affords;
Sweet playful phrases, which would seem absurd
To those who have ceased to hear such, or ne'er heard.

XV

All these were theirs, for they were children still,
   And children still they should have ever been;
They were not made in the real world to fill
   A busy character in the dull scene,
But like two beings born from out a rill,
   A nymph and her beloved, all unseen
To pass their lives in fountains and on flowers,
And never know the weight of human hours.

XVI

Moons changing had roll'd on, and changeless found
   Those their bright rise had lighted to such joys
As rarely they beheld throughout their round;
   And these were not of the vain kind which cloys,
For theirs were buoyant spirits, never bound
   By the mere senses; and that which destroys
Most love, possession, unto them appear'd
A thing which each endearment more endear'd.

XVII

Oh beautiful! and rare as beautiful!
   But theirs was love in which the mind delights
To lose itself, when the old world grows dull,
   And we are sick of its hack sounds and sights,
Intrigues, adventures of the common school,
   Its petty passions, marriages, and flights,
Where Hymen's torch but brands one strumpet more,
Whose husband only knows her not a wh—re.

XVIII

Hard words; harsh truth; a truth which many know.
  Enough.—The faithful and the fairy pair,
Who never found a single hour too slow,
  What was it made them thus exempt from care?
Young innate feelings all have felt below,
  Which perish in the rest, but in them were
Inherent; what we mortals call romantic,
And always envy, though we deem it frantic.

XIX

This is in others a factitious state,
  An opium dream of too much youth and reading,
But was in them their nature or their fate:
  No novels e'er had set their young hearts bleeding,
For Haidée's knowledge was by no means great,
  And Juan was a boy of saintly breeding;
So that there was no reason for their loves
More than for those of nightingales or doves.

XX

They gazed upon the sunset; 'tis an hour
  Dear unto all, but dearest to *their* eyes,
For it had made them what they were: the power
  Of love had first o'erwhelm'd them from such skies,
When happiness had been their only dower,
  And twilight saw them link'd in passion's ties;
Charm'd with each other, all things charm'd that brought
The past still welcome as the present thought.

XXI

I know not why, but in that hour to-night,
  Even as they gazed, a sudden tremor came,
And swept, as 'twere, across their hearts' delight,
  Like the wind o'er a harp-string, or a flame,

When one is shook in sound, and one in sight:
   And thus some boding flash'd through either frame,
And call'd from Juan's breast a faint low sigh,
While one new tear arose in Haidée's eye.

XXII

That large black prophet eye seem'd to dilate
   And follow far the disappearing sun,
As if their last day of a happy date
   With his broad, bright, and dropping orb were gone,
Juan gazed on her as to ask his fate—
   He felt a grief, but knowing cause for none,
His glance inquired of hers for some excuse
For feelings causeless, or at least abstruse.

XXIII

She turn'd to him, and smiled, but in that sort
   Which makes not others smile; then turn'd aside:
Whatever feeling shook her, it seem'd short,
   And master'd by her wisdom or her pride;
When Juan spoke, too—it might be in sport—
   Of this their mutual feeling, she replied—
'If it should be so,—but—it cannot be—
Or I at least shall not survive to see.'

XXIV

Juan would question further, but she press'd
   His lips to hers, and silenced him with this,
And then dismiss'd the omen from her breast,
   Defying augury with that fond kiss;
And no doubt of all methods 'tis the best:
   Some people prefer wine—'tis not amiss;
I have tried both; so those who would a part take
May choose between the headache and the heartache.

XXV

One of the two, according to your choice,
   Woman or wine, you'll have to undergo;
Both maladies are taxes on our joys:
   But which to choose, I really hardly know;
And if I had to give a casting voice,
   For both sides I could many reasons show,
And then decide, without great wrong to either,
It were much better to have both than neither.

XXVI

Juan and Haidée gazed upon each other
   With swimming looks of speechless tenderness,
Which mix'd all feelings, friend, child, lover, brother;
   All that the best can mingle and express
When two pure hearts are pour'd in one another,
   And love too much, and yet cannot love less;
But almost sanctify the sweet excess
By the immortal wish and power to bless.

XXVII

Mix'd in each other's arms, and heart in heart,
   Why did they not then die?—they had lived too long
Should an hour come to bid them breathe apart;
   Years could but bring them cruel things or wrong;
The world was not for them, nor the world's art
   For beings passionate as Sappho's song;
Love was born *with* them, *in* them, so intense,
It was their very spirit—not a sense.

XXVIII

They should have lived together deep in woods,
   Unseen as sings the nightingale; they were
Unfit to mix in these thick solitudes
   Call'd social, haunts of Hate, and Vice, and Care;

How lonely every freeborn creature broods!
    The sweetest song-birds nestle in a pair;
The eagle soars alone; the gull and crow
Flock o'er their carrion, just like men below.

XXIX

Now pillow'd cheek to cheek, in loving sleep,
    Haidée and Juan their siesta took,
A gentle slumber, but it was not deep,
    For ever and anon a something shook
Juan, and shuddering o'er his frame would creep;
    And Haidée's sweet lips murmur'd like a brook
A wordless music, and her face so fair
Stirr'd with her dream, as rose-leaves with the air;

XXX

Or as the stirring of a deep clear stream
    Within an Alpine hollow, when the wind
Walks o'er it, was she shaken by the dream,
    The mystical usurper of the mind—
O'erpowering us to be whate'er may seem
    Good to the soul which we no more can bind:
Strange state of being! (for 'tis still to be),
Senseless to feel, and with seal'd eyes to see.

XXXI

She dream'd of being alone on the sea-shore,
    Chain'd to a rock; she knew not how, but stir
She could not from the spot, and the loud roar
    Grew, and each wave rose roughly, threatening her;
And o'er her upper lip they seem'd to pour,
    Until she sobb'd for breath, and soon they were
Foaming o'er her lone head, so fierce and high—
Each broke to drown her, yet she could not die.

XXXII

Anon—she was released, and then she stray'd
  O'er the sharp shingles with her bleeding feet,
And stumbled almost every step she made;
  And something roll'd before her in a sheet,
Which she must still pursue howe'er afraid:
  'Twas white and indistinct, nor stopp'd to meet
Her glance nor grasp, for she still gazed and grasp'd,
And ran, but it escaped her as she clasp'd.

XXXIII

The dream changed:—in a cave she stood, its walls
  Were hung with marble icicles; the work
Of ages on its water-fretted halls,
  Where waves might wash, and seals might breed and
    lurk;
Her hair was dripping, and the very balls
  Of her black eyes seem'd turn'd to tears, and mirk
The sharp rocks look'd below each drop they caught,
Which froze to marble as it fell, she thought.

XXXIV

And wet, and cold, and lifeless at her feet,
  Pale as the foam that froth'd on his dead brow,
Which she essay'd in vain to clear, (how sweet
  Were once her cares, how idle seem'd they now!)
Lay Juan, nor could aught renew the beat
  Of his quench'd heart; and the sea dirges low
Rang in her sad ears like a mermaid's song,
And that brief dream appear'd a life too long.

XXXV

And gazing on the dead, she thought his face
  Faded, or alter'd into something new—
Like to her father's features, till each trace
  More like and like to Lambro's aspect grew—

With all his keen worn look and Grecian grace;
   And starting, she awoke, and what to view?
Oh! Powers of Heaven! what dark eye meets she there?
'Tis—'tis her father's—fixed upon the pair!

XXXVI

Then shrieking, she arose, and shrieking fell,
   With joy and sorrow, hope and fear, to see
Him whom she deem'd a habitant where dwell
   The ocean-buried, risen from death, to be
Perchance the death of one she loved too well:
   Dear as her father had been to Haidée,
It was a moment of that awful kind——
I have seen such—but must not call to mind.

XXXVII

Up Juan sprung to Haidée's bitter shriek,
   And caught her falling, and from off the wall
Snatch'd down his sabre, in hot haste to wreak
   Vengeance on him who was the cause of all:
Then Lambro, who till now forbore to speak,
   Smiled scornfully, and said, 'Within my call,
A thousand scimitars await the word;
Put up, young man, put up your silly sword.'

XXXVIII

And Haidée clung around him; 'Juan, 'tis—
   'Tis Lambro—'tis my father! Kneel with me—
He will forgive us—yes—it must be—yes.
   Oh! dearest father, in this agony
Of pleasure and of pain—even while I kiss
   Thy garment's hem with transport, can it be
That doubt should mingle with my filial joy?
Deal with me as thou wilt, but spare this boy.'

XXXIX

High and inscrutable the old man stood,
    Calm in his voice, and calm within his eye—
Not always signs with him of calmest mood:
    He look'd upon her, but gave no reply;
Then turn'd to Juan, in whose cheek the blood
    Oft came and went, as there resolved to die;
In arms, at least, he stood, in act to spring
On the first foe whom Lambro's call might bring.

XL

'Young man, your sword;' so Lambro once more said:
    Juan replied, 'Not while this arm is free.'
The old man's cheek grew pale, but not with dread,
    And drawing from his belt a pistol, he
Replied, 'Your blood be then on your own head.'
    Then look'd close at the flint, as if to see
'Twas fresh—for he had lately used the lock—
And next proceeded quietly to cock.

XLI

It has a strange quick jar upon the ear,
    That cocking of a pistol, when you know
A moment more will bring the sight to bear
    Upon your person, twelve yards off, or so;
A gentlemanly distance, not too near,
    If you have got a former friend for foe;
But after being fired at once or twice,
The ear becomes more Irish, and less nice.

XLII

Lambro presented, and one instant more
    Had stopp'd this Canto, and Don Juan's breath,
When Haidée threw herself her boy before;
    Stern as her sire: 'On me,' she cried, 'let death

Descend—the fault is mine; this fatal shore
   He found—but sought not. I have pledged my faith;
I love him—I will die with him: I knew
Your nature's firmness—know your daughter's too.'

XLIII

A minute past, and she had been all tears,
   And tenderness, and infancy; but now
She stood as one who champion'd human fears—
   Pale, statue-like, and stern, she woo'd the blow;
And tall beyond her sex, and their compeers,
   She drew up to her height, as if to show
A fairer mark; and with a fix'd eye scann'd
Her father's face—but never stopp'd his hand.

XLIV

He gazed on her, and she on him; 'twas strange
   How like they look'd! the expression was the same;
Serenely savage, with a little change
   In the large dark eye's mutual-darted flame;
For she, too, was as one who could avenge,
   If cause should be—a lioness, though tame;
Her father's blood before her father's face
Boil'd up, and proved her truly of his race.

XLV

I said they were alike, their features and
   Their stature, differing but in sex and years;
Even to the delicacy of their hand
   There was resemblance, such as true blood wears;
And now to see them, thus divided, stand
   In fix'd ferocity, when joyous tears,
And sweet sensations, should have welcomed both,
Show what the passions are in their full growth.

M

XLVI

The father paused a moment, then withdrew
  His weapon, and replaced it; but stood still,
And looking on her, as to look her through,
  'Not *I*,' he said, 'have sought this stranger's ill;
Not *I* have made this desolation: few
  Would bear such outrage, and forbear to kill;
But I must do my duty—how thou hast
Done thine, the present vouches for the past.

XLVII

'Let him disarm; or, by my father's head,
  His own shall roll before you like a ball!'
He raised his whistle as the word he said,
  And blew; another answer'd to the call,
And rushing in disorderly, though led,
  And arm'd from boot to turban, one and all,
Some twenty of his train came, rank on rank;
He gave the word, 'Arrest or slay the Frank.'

XLVIII

Then, with a sudden movement, he withdrew
  His daughter; while compress'd within his clasp,
'Twixt her and Juan interposed the crew;
  In vain she struggled in her father's grasp—
His arms were like a serpent's coil: then flew
  Upon their prey, as darts an angry asp,
The file of pirates: save the foremost, who
Had fallen, with his right shoulder half cut through.

XLIX

The second had his cheek laid open; but
  The third, a wary, cool old sworder, took
The blows upon his cutlass, and then put
  His own well in; so well ere you could look,

His man was floor'd, and helpless at his foot,
    With the blood running like a little brook
From two smart sabre gashes, deep and red—
One on the arm, the other on the head.

L

And then they bound him where he fell, and bore
    Juan from the apartment: with a sign
Old Lambro bade them take him to the shore,
    Where lay some ships which were to sail at nine.
They laid him in a boat, and plied the oar
    Until they reach'd some galliots, placed in line;
On board of one of these, and under hatches,
They stow'd him, with strict orders to the watches.

LI

The world is full of strange vicissitudes,
    And here was one exceedingly unpleasant:
A gentleman so rich in the world's goods,
    Handsome and young, enjoying all the present,
Just at the very time when he least broods
    On such a thing, is suddenly to sea sent,
Wounded and chain'd, so that he cannot move,
And all because a lady fell in love.

LII

Here I must leave him, for I grow pathetic,
    Moved by the Chinese nymph of tears, green tea!
Than whom Cassandra was not more prophetic;
    For if my pure libations exceed three,
I feel my heart become so sympathetic,
    That I must have recourse to black Bohea:
'Tis pity wine should be so deleterious,
For tea and coffee leaves us much more serious,

LIII

Unless when qualified with thee, Cogniac!
  Sweet Naïad of the Phlegethontic rill!
Ah! why the liver wilt thou thus attack,
  And make, like other nymphs, thy lovers ill?
I would take refuge in weak punch, but *rack*
  (In each sense of the word), whene'er I fill
My mild and midnight beakers to the brim,
Wakes me next morning with its synonym.

LIV

I leave Don Juan for the present, safe—
  Not sound, poor fellow, but severely wounded;
Yet could his corporal pangs amount to half
  Of those with which his Haidée's bosom bounded!
She was not one to weep, and rave, and chafe,
  And then give way, subdued because surrounded;
Her mother was a Moorish maid from Fez,
Where all is Eden, or a wilderness.

LV

There the large olive rains its amber store
  In marble fonts; there grain, and flour, and fruit,
Gush from the earth until the land runs o'er;
  But there, too, many a poison-tree has root,
And midnight listens to the lion's roar,
  And long, long deserts scorch the camel's foot,
Or heaving whelm the helpless caravan;
And as the soil is, so the heart of man.

LVI

Afric is all the sun's, and as her earth
  Her human clay is kindled; full of power
For good or evil, burning from its birth,
  The Moorish blood partakes the planet's hour,

And like the soil beneath it will bring forth:
  Beauty and love were Haidée's mother's dower;
But her large dark eye show'd deep Passion's force,
Though sleeping like a lion near a source.

                            LVII

Her daughter, temper'd with a milder ray,
  Like summer clouds all silvery, smooth, and fair,
Till slowly charged with thunder they display
  Terror to earth, and tempest to the air,
Had held till now her soft and milky way;
  But overwrought with passion and despair,
The fire burst forth from her Numidian veins,
Even as the Simoom sweeps the blasted plains.

                            LVIII

The last sight which she saw was Juan's gore,
  And he himself o'ermaster'd and cut down;
His blood was running on the very floor
  Where late he trod, her beautiful, her own;
Thus much she view'd an instant and no more,—
  Her struggles ceased with one convulsive groan;
On her sire's arm, which until now scarce held
Her writhing, fell she like a cedar fell'd.

                            LIX

A vein had burst, and her sweet lips' pure dyes
  Were dabbled with the deep blood which ran o'er;
And her head droop'd, as when the lily lies
  O'ercharged with rain: her summon'd handmaids bore
Their lady to her couch with gushing eyes;
  Of herbs and cordials they produced their store,
But she defied all means they could employ,
Like one life could not hold, nor death destroy.

LX

Days lay she in that state unchanged, though chill—
  With nothing livid, still her lips were red;
She had no pulse, but death seem'd absent still;
  No hideous sign proclaim'd her surely dead;
Corruption came not in each mind to kill
  All hope; to look upon her sweet face bred
New thoughts of life, for it seem'd full of soul—
She had so much, earth could not claim the whole.

LXI

The ruling passion, such as marble shows
  When exquisitely chisell'd, still lay there,
But fix'd as marble's unchanged aspect throws
  O'er the fair Venus, but for ever fair;
O'er the Laocoön's all eternal throes,
  And ever-dying Gladiator's air,
Their energy like life forms all their fame,
Yet looks not life, for they are still the same.

LXII

She woke at length, but not as sleepers wake,
  Rather the dead, for life seem'd something new,
A strange sensation which she must partake
  Perforce, since whatsoever met her view
Struck not on memory, though a heavy ache
  Lay at her heart, whose earliest beat still true
Brought back the sense of pain without the cause,
For, for a while, the furies made a pause.

LXIII

She look'd on many a face with vacant eye,
  On many a token without knowing what;
She saw them watch her without asking why,
  And reck'd not who around her pillow sat;

Not speechless, though she spoke not; not a sigh
    Relieved her thoughts; dull silence and quick chat
Were tried in vain by those who served; she gave
No sign, save breath, of having left the grave.

LXIV

Her handmaids tended, but she heeded not;
    Her father watch'd, she turn'd her eyes away;
She recognised no being, and no spot,
    However dear or cherish'd in their day;
They changed from room to room, but all forgot,
    Gentle, but without memory she lay;
At length those eyes, which they would fain be weaning
Back to old thoughts, wax'd full of fearful meaning.

LXV

And then a slave bethought her of a harp;
    The harper came, and tuned his instrument;
At the first notes, irregular and sharp,
    On him her flashing eyes a moment bent,
Then to the wall she turn'd as if to warp
    Her thoughts from sorrow through her heart re-sent;
And he began a long low island song
Of ancient days, ere tyranny grew strong.

LXVI

Anon her thin wan fingers beat the wall
    In time to his old tune; he changed the theme,
And sung of love; the fierce name struck through all
    Her recollection; on her flash'd the dream
Of what she was, and is, if ye could call
    To be so being; in a gushing stream
The tears rush'd forth from her o'erclouded brain,
Like mountain mists at length dissolved in rain.

LXVII

Short solace, vain relief!—thought came too quick,
   And whirl'd her brain to madness; she arose
As one who ne'er had dwelt among the sick,
   And flew at all she met, as on her foes;
But no one ever heard her speak or shriek,
   Although her paroxysm drew towards its close;—
Hers was a phrensy which disdain'd to rave,
Even when they smote her, in the hope to save.

LXVIII

Yet she betray'd at times a gleam of sense;
   Nothing could make her meet her father's face,
Though on all other things with looks intense
   She gazed but none she ever could retrace;
Food she refused, and raiment; no pretence
   Avail'd for either; neither change of place,
Nor time, nor skill, nor remedy, could give her
Senses to sleep—the power seem'd gone for ever.

LXIX

Twelve days and nights she wither'd thus; at last,
   Without a groan, or sigh, or glance, to show
A parting pang, the spirit from her passed:
   And they who watch'd her nearest could not know
The very instant, till the change that cast
   Her sweet face into shadow, dull and slow,
Glazed o'er her eyes—the beautiful, the black—
Oh! to possess such lustre—and then lack!

LXX

She died, but not alone; she held within
   A second principle of life, which might
Have dawn'd a fair and sinless child of sin;
   But closed its little being without light,

And went down to the grave unborn, wherein
   Blossom and bough lie wither'd with one blight;
In vain the dews of Heaven descend above
The bleeding flower and blasted fruit of love.

LXXI

Thus lived—thus died she; never more on her
   Shall sorrow light, or shame. She was not made
Through years or moons the inner weight to bear,
   Which colder hearts endure till they are laid
By age in earth; her days and pleasures were
   Brief, but delightful—such as had not staid
Long with her destiny; but she sleeps well
By the sea-shore, whereon she loved to dwell.

NOTES TO THE POEM

I. 1. Southey accepted the laureateship in 1813 on the death of Henry James Pye.

I. 6. The Lakers, or Lake Poets, so called from their residence in, or association with, the Lake District, were Southey, Wordsworth, and Coleridge.

IV. 1. *The Excursion*, in nine Books, amounting to nearly 9,000 lines, appeared in 1814. 'It is not the Author's intention formally to announce a system,' Wordsworth wrote in the Preface; but 'the Reader will have no difficulty in extracting the system for himself.'

IV. 6. *dog-star*: Sirius, the brightest star in the firmament, whose influence, according to classical writers, caused great heat in summer.

VI. 6. Wordsworth was appointed distributor of stamps for the County of Westmorland in 1813.

VII. 7. The poets contemporary with Byron whom he most admired.

VIII. 2. An allusion to Pegasus, the winged steed whose name is synonymous with poetic inspiration.

IX. 1. *laurels for posterity*: cf. the final stanza of Canto I.

IX. 6. *Titan*, as Virgil and Ovid sometimes named the sun-god, rose from the sea in the morning, drove his chariot across the sky, and in the evening descended to the sea in the west.

X. 1–2. Cf. *Par. Lost*, VII. 25–26: '. . . though fall'n on evil days,/On evil days though fall'n, and evil tongues.'

XI. 2. Cf. I. *Samuel*, 28. 13–14.

XI. 6. 'Milton's two elder daughters are said to have robbed him of his books, besides cheating and plaguing him in the economy of his house, &c. &c.' (Byron).

XI. 8. Robert Stewart, Viscount Castlereagh (1769–1822), one of Byron's *bêtes noires* (cf. Shelley, *The Mask of Anarchy*: 'I met

Murder on the way—/He had a mask like Castlereagh—').
Foreign Secretary (1812–22), opponent of liberal policies both
in England and in Europe.

XII. 2. *Erin's gore*: as chief Secretary for Ireland (1799–1801),
Castlereagh repressed the United Irish rebellion, and secured
the passing of the Act of Union by the Irish parliament.

XII. 7–8. *fetters . . . fixed*: Castlereagh supported Austria's claims
in Italy—as a tool of Metternich, in the opinion of some
people.

XIII. 1. *orator*: Castlereagh's speeches were often confused and
ineptly phrased.

XIII. 6. *Ixion*: in Greek legend, a king of the Lapithae, bound to a
revolving wheel of fire in the infernal regions, either for
imitating the thunder of Zeus, or for boasting of the favours of
Hera.

XIV. 5. *Conspiracy or Congress*: referring to the treaties after the
downfall of Napoleon which Byron regarded as betrayals of the
liberty of European peoples.

XV. 5. *Eutropius*, 'one of the principal eunuchs of the palace of
Constantinople', became a Roman magistrate and general
(A.D. 395); see Gibbon, *Decline and Fall*, Chap. XXIX.

XVI. 2–5. In 1814 an English expedition drove the French from
Genoa and placed it under the control of its hated rival Sar-
dinia; this was apparently done with Castlereagh's knowledge,
although later, at the Congress of Vienna, he supported the
annexation of Genoa to Piedmont.

XVII. 4. 'Mr. Fox and the Whig Club of his time adopted an
uniform of blue and buff: hence the coverings of the Edinburgh Review, &c.' (Moore).

XVII. 8. Julian the Apostate, Roman emperor (A.D. 361–3),
nephew of Constantine the Great, was brought up as a
Christian; he repudiated Christianity on his accession.

CANTO I

I. 7. *Pantomime*: it is not known to which of the many dramatic
or quasi-dramatic versions of the Don Juan story Byron is
referring; perhaps to no one particular version. See Introd.,
pp. xvi–xiiv.

II. 1–7. *Vernon . . . Demourier*: naval and military leaders of the
period, English and French.

II. 5–6. See *Macbeth*, IV, i. 112 ff., 64–5.

II. 8. *Moniteur . . . Courier*: French newspapers.

III. 1–2. *Barnave . . . La Fayette*: leaders and thinkers of the French Revolution.

III. 5. *Joubert . . . Moreau*: French military leaders.

IV. 8. *Duncan . . . Jervis*: English admirals.

V. i. 'Vixere fortes ante Agamemnona/multi' (Horace, *Odes* IV. ix. 25–6).

VI. In the *Ars Poetica* (148–9) Horace discusses the most effective way in which a poet may begin an epic: '. . . in medias res/non secus ac notas auditorem rapit' ('he plunges his hearer into the middle of the story as if it were already familiar to him'). Thus in Book I of the *Aeneid* Aeneas's ships are driven on to the shores of Libya; he is royally entertained by Dido, Queen of Carthage, and 'at his ease' after a feast he recounts 'what went before—by way of episode': the destruction of Troy and his subsequent adventures (Bks. II and III). In Bk. IV Aeneas and Dido take refuge from a storm in a cavern. In the *Odyssey*, too, earlier events of the story are sometimes narrated retrospectively after feasts.

VIII. 4. *the proverb*: 'Quien no ha visto Sevilla/No ha visto maravilla' ('He who has not seen Seville has missed seeing a marvel').

IX. 2. *Hidalgo*: A Spanish gentleman of birth; one of the lower nobility.

IX. 4. *Gothic gentlemen of Spain*: The Visigoths, the last and the most civilised of the Germanic peoples who entered Spain at the break-up of the Roman Empire in the west, came in early in the 5th cent., and by the middle of the century controlled the whole peninsula. The Visigothic kingdom was overthrown by the Moorish invasion in A.D. 711. By then there had been much intermarriage between Visigoths and Romanised Spaniards, especially at the level of the nobility. To claim Gothic descent in Spain was not unlike claiming Norman descent in England. In the middle ages there was a large Jewish population in Spain; intermarriage between Spaniards and Jews was frowned on, but often took place.

X. 1. *learned lady*: In spite of Byron's early disclaimers, Donna Inez is clearly to some extent a satirical portrait of his wife. 'When Lord Byron was praising the mental and personal qualifications of Lady Byron, I asked him how all that he now said agreed with certain sarcasms supposed to bear a reference to her, in his works. He smiled, shook his head, and said they were meant to spite and vex her, when he was wounded and irritated at her refusing to receive or answer his letters; that he was not sincere in his implied censures, and that he was sorry he had written them' (Lady Blessington, *Conversations with Lord Byron*, 1834).

XI. 2. Pedro Calderón de la Barca (1600–81) and Lope Félix de Vega Carpio (1562–1635), great Spanish playwrights.

XI. 5. Professor Gregor von Feinagle, of Baden, in 1812 'delivered a course of lectures at the Royal Institution, on Mnemonics' (Moore).

XII. 3. *Attic*: The Athenians were noted for the elegance of their wit, or 'salt', though Byron is probably here referring mockingly to the learned nature of his wife's wit.

XV. 4. Sir Samuel Romilly, Solicitor General 1806–7, committed suicide in 1818 after his wife's death. Byron had paid him a retaining fee to represent him against Lady Byron in the separation proceedings, but Romilly went over to Lady Byron, for which Byron never forgave him.

XVI. 2–4. Maria Edgeworth (1767–1849), co-author with her father of *Practical Education*, author of moral novels and tales and of novels about Irish life. Sarah Trimmer (1741–1810), author of *Guardian to Education* and of other educational and moral works. *Coelebs in Search of a Wife*, by Hannah More (1745–1833), is a series of social sketches and precepts drawn together as the plot of a novel in which the hero tries to find a wife possessing the qualities laid down as desirable by his dead parents. Moore describes it as 'a sermonlike novel'.

XVI. 7. 'If to her share some female errors fall,/Look on her face, and you'll forget 'em all' (Pope, *Rape of the Lock*, II. 17–18).

XVII. 6. John Harrison (1693–1776), a famous clock-maker.

XVII. 8. 'Description des *vertus incomparables* de l'Huile de Macassar. See the Advertisement' (Byron). Macassar oil was used as a hair-dressing.

XXI. 5. "Zouns, an I were now by this rascal, I could brain him with his lady's fan' (*1 Henry IV*, II. iii. 22–4).

XXVI–XXVII. Byron is recalling the break-up of his own marriage. 'Previously to my departure, it had been strongly impressed on my mind, that Lord Byron was under the influence of *insanity*. . . . *With the concurrence of his family*, I had consulted Dr.

Baillie as a friend (Jan. 8th) respecting this supposed malady'
(Lady Byron, quoted by Moore).

XXVIII–XXXI. The omitted stanzas give further details of the
quarrel.

XLII–XLIV. No doubt Byron has in mind Ovid's *Ars Amatoria*
and *Amores*, and perhaps some of his elegies; the amatory
verse of Anacreon (6th cent. B.C.), or more probably, since only
fragments of this survive, the later imitations known as the
Anacreontea; Catullus's poems to Lesbia, at first full of
passionate love but later of virulent insults; the ode by Sappho
(7th cent. B.C.) which Longinus (1st cent. A.D.) quotes in his
treatise *On the Sublime* as an example of sublimity of expression. Virgil's second Eclogue, in which one shepherd 'burns'
with love for another, opens with the words '*Formosum pastor
Corydon*'. A leading purpose of Lucretius in *De Rerum Natura*,
in which he expounds the atomic theory as laid down by
Epicurus, and aims at demonstrating that natural phenomena
have natural causes, is to combat the superstitious reverence of
his countrymen for the gods—hence his 'irreligion'. The satires
of Juvenal denounce in downright and sometimes coarse terms
the vices of Rome in 1st cent. A.D. Many of the epigrams of
Martial, an older contemporary of Juvenal, are decidedly in-
delicate. On *in an appendix* Byron gives a note: 'Fact. There is,
or was, such an edition, with all the obnoxious epigrams of
Martial placed by themselves at the end.' He may be referring
to an edition published at Amsterdam in 1701, and dedicated
to the young Dauphin of France, in which all the 'nauseous'
epigrams were printed at the end.

XLV–XLVI. Of the omitted stanzas the first further describes the
edition which places the indecent passages where 'we have
them all "at one fell swoop"'; the second describes the illu-
minated family Missal, which was ornamented with amorous
drawings—'But Don Juan's mother/Kept this herself, and
gave her son another.'

XLVII. *St Jerome* (c. A.D. 340–420), best known as the translator
of the Bible into the Latin version known as the Vulgate, also
wrote Scriptural commentaries and lives of early Christian
writers and hermits. *St. John Chrysostom* (c. A.D. 345–407), the
most prominent of the Greek Fathers of the Church, wrote
homilies and Scriptural commentaries; like St. Jerome, he was
an ascetic. *St. Augustine* of Hippo (A.D. 345–430) wrote many

works, of which the most famous is *The City of God*; in his *Confessions* he gives a striking account of his wild early life and his conversion.

LIII. 4. 'Verbum satis sapienti' ('A word to the wise is enough').

LVI. 5–6. The Kingdom of Granada, the last of the Moorish possessions in Spain, was conquered by Ferdinand and Isabella after a long war (1482–92). Its conquest is the subject of a play by Dryden and of a romantic history in satirical vein by Washington Irving. The Moorish king Boabdil is said to have wept as he gazed from a hill at his conquered capital.

LXII–CXCI. Juan's *affaire* with the Donna Julia is based on fact. In a letter to Hobhouse Byron wrote: 'The *Julian* adventure detailed was none of mine; but one of an acquaintance of mine (Parôlini by name), which happened some years ago at Bassano, with the Prefect's wife, when he was a boy; and was the subject of a long case, ending in a divorce or separation of the parties during the Italian Viceroyalty.'

LXII. 6. *"mi vien in mente"*: 'it comes into my mind'.

LXIV. The omitted stanza describes as a contrast the 'moral north', where the coldness of the weather promotes virtue.

LXXI. 7. In Tasso's *Jerusalem Delivered* Armida, niece of the King of Damascus, by her beauty lures away many of the great Christian knights who are besieging Jerusalem; using magic powers, she entices them into a delightful garden, where they are overcome by indolence.

LXXV. 6. Tarquinius Superbus, noted for his arrogance and tyranny, was the last of the seven legendary kings of Rome. His son Sextus ravished the virtuous Lucretia, an outrage which led to the expulsion of the Tarquins from Rome. See Shakespeare's *Rape of Lucrece*.

LXXVIII–LXXX. The omitted stanzas are a digression on 'Platonic' love.

LXXXVI. 4. In Bk. VIII of Ovid's *Metamorphoses* Medea puzzles over the new feelings kindled in her by the knowledge that Jason will almost certainly be killed in his attempt to win the Golden Fleece. Realizing that she is in love with him, she decides to help him to overcome the obstacles placed in his path by her father.

LXXXVIII–LXXXIX. The omitted stanzas contain a quotation on love from Campbell's *Gertrude of Wyoming* and Byron's reflections on it.

XCII. 6. There were several attempts, fairly successful ones by Sir George Cayley and Charles Green, to make navigable air-balloons in early 19th-cent. England.

XCIV–XCVI. Further details of Juan's 'lonely walks and lengthening reveries'.

XCVIII–C. Reflections on the short-sightedness of parents in contrast to the jealous vigilance of husbands.

CIV. 5. Byron's friend Thomas Moore, the poet, translated (1800) the *Anacreontea*, wrongly believed to be genuine odes by Anacreon. The reference to Mahomet may allude to Moore's tale of 'Paradise and the Peri' in *Lalla Rookh* (1817).

CXVI. 1. Platonic love is spiritual, non-sexual love between men and women. The phrase takes its rise from a passage in the *Symposium* in which Plato is in fact extolling the spiritual love of Socrates for young men. For Byron's sentiments cf. Richardson, *Pamela*, I. lxxviii: 'I am convinced, and always was, that Platonic Love is Platonic nonsense.'

CXVIII–CXIX. A digression of pleasure.

CXX. 7. Aristotle laid down no rules of composition in his *Poetics*; he described and discussed the practice of Greek dramatic and epic poets. Renaissance critics formulated some of his comments as rules.

CXXV. 4. 'They hate us youth' (Falstaff in *1 Henry IV*, II. ii. 93). It has been suggested that in this line Byron is referring to his mother.

CXXV. 8. A post-obit bond is an agreement to repay a loan after the death of a specified person; it usually entails a high rate of interest. Post-obit obligations that Byron incurred at Cambridge contributed for some years to his financial troubles.

CXXVIII–CXXXII. A satirical digression on the theme, 'Man's a strange animal'.

CXXXVIII. 6. A cuckold, or husband whose wife takes a lover, is traditionally said to wear horns, or to be presented with a pair of horns.

CXLVII–CLII. Six stanzas containing further vigorous protestations of unassailable virtue and injured innocence have been omitted.

CLIX. 6. 'Fidus Achates', the faithful friend and attendant of Virgil's Aeneas.

CLXII. 6. 'Thou speakest as one of the foolish women speaketh' (*Book of Job*, 2.10).

CLXIV. I. '*posse comitatus*': body of supporters; literally, the power or force of the county—all males over fifteen, who may be summoned by the sheriff to assist in preventing disorders.

CLXIV. 5. '*hiatus*': gap.

CLXV. 5. 'But he that filches from me my good name/Robs me of that which not enriches him/And makes me poor indeed' (Iago in *Othello*, III. iii. 160–2).

CLXVI. 8. 'I'll drown you in the malmsey-butt within' (Murderer in *Richard III*, I. iv. 270).

CLXVIII. 2–8. See I *Kings*, I. 1–4.

CLXXX. 5. Cf. *Paradise Lost*, XII. 638: 'Our ling'ring parents'.

CLXXXIII. 4. An income tax was imposed as a war tax in 1799, but not again until 1842.

CLXXXVI. 7. When Joseph was importuned by Potiphar's wife to lie with her, 'he left his garment in her hand, and fled, and got him out' (*Genesis*, 39. 12).

CLXXXVIII. 8. The separation proceedings of Byron and his wife were sensationally reported in the newspapers.

CLXXXIX. 7. W. B. Gurney, shorthand writer to the Houses of Parliament, reported also on other matters of public interest.

CXC. 4. *Vandals*: A Teutonic race from the Baltic which in the 5th cent. ravaged Gaul and sacked Rome.

CXCVIII. 6. 'She follows you everywhere', the motto on Byron's own seal.

CC. I. Medwin, in his *Conversations with Lord Byron*, quotes Byron as saying: 'If you must have an epic, there's *Don Juan* for you. I call that an epic: it is an epic as much in the spirit of our day as the Iliad was in Homer's.' Byron goes on to describe the epic qualities of the poem.

CC. 6. In many versions of the Don Juan story the hero is at the end carried off to Hell by devils. In Feb. 1816 Byron wrote to his publisher, John Murray: 'I had not quite fixed whether to make him end in Hell or in an unhappy marriage, not knowing which would be the severest.'

CCI. 3. *vade mecum*: literally, 'go with me'; used for a handbook containing much useful information in small compass.

CCI. 7. Supernatural beings who take part in the action of an epic are called the machinery.

CCII. 8. *actually true*: Byron prided himself on always having some factual basis for his poetry, whether from his own experience or from his reading. In April 1817 he wrote to

N

Murray: 'There should always be some foundation of fact for the most airy fabric, and pure invention is but the talent of a liar.'

CCIII. 4–8. See Introd., pp. xvi–xvii. It is possible that Byron saw a Don Juan play in Spain, perhaps *E Burlador de Sevilla*.

CCIV. 2. *commandments*: many contemporaries regarded Byron's parody of the Ten Commandments as blasphemous; he himself was a little worried lest his 'foolish jest' should affect his rights as guardian of his daughter.

CCIV. 7–8. Longinus's treatise *On the Sublime* (1st cent. A.D.) and Aristotle's *Poetics* (4th cent. B.C.) were regarded as authoritative guides to literary composition.

CCV. 5–8. Byron admired the poetry of George Crabbe (1754–1832), whom he described in *English Bards* as 'nature's sternest painter, yet the best', and of Thomas Campbell (1777–1844). Campbell's Muse might be regarded as 'somewhat drouthy' because he had recently turned from poetry to criticism. Samuel Rogers (1763–1855) and Thomas Moore (1779–1852) were other poets, and friends, whom Byron esteemed highly. Hippocrene ('fountain of the horse') was a spring on Mt. Helicon, said to have been produced by a stroke of the hoof of Pegasus; the name is used as a synonym for poetic inspiration.

CCVI. 1–2. William Sotheby (1757–1833), translator of Virgil's *Georgics*, the *Iliad*, and the *Odyssey*. In *English Bards* Byron named him as one of the 'genuine sons' of Poesy, but in the belief that Sotheby was the writer of an impertinent anonymous letter that he received and of disparaging marginal comments in a copy of *The Prisoner of Chillon and Other Poems*, he turned against him, and satirised him as 'Botherby' in *Beppo*, and later in *The Blues* (1823).

CCVI. 3. '*the Blues*': in many letters (and in *The Blues*) Byron ridiculed what he regarded as the false pretensions of the Bluestockings, i.e., female *savants* or pedants. The original Bluestockings, so called from the colour of their stockings, were a society of ladies and gentlemen formed at Venice in 1400. In France in the late 16th and England in the late 18th cent., the term was applied to (or adopted by) ladies who held literary *soirées*.

CCVII. 2. Byron always insisted that *Don Juan* was not an immoral poem.

CCIX. 8. *the British*: the *British Review*, whose editor, William Roberts, took Byron's joke seriously and published a disclaimer.

CCX–CCXXI. The (regretfully) omitted stanzas contain half-rueful, half-amused reflections on Byron's disillusion now that he has reached the age of thirty, and on ambition and fame.

CCXXII. 1–4. From the last stanza of Southey's *Epilogue to the Lay of the Laureate*.

CANTO II

V. 4. The Spaniards under Pizarro had conquered Peru in 1531. Now in revolt, the Peruvians gained their independence in 1821.

VI–VII. Further description of the 'sweet girls' of Cadiz.

XVI. 1–2. 'By the rivers of Babylon, there we sat down, yea, we wept, when we remembered Zion' (*Psalm* 137. 1).

XVII. 3. '*Sweets to the sweet*': See *Hamlet*, V. i. 265.

XXII–XXIII. A digression on love and the effect on it of various illnesses.

XXIV–CIV. For his descriptions of the storm, the shipwreck, the calm, and the 'cannibal' episode Byron drew very extensively on authentic narratives. Most of these he read in *Shipwrecks and Disasters at Sea*, a large collection of such narratives ed. by Sir J. G. Dalyell (1812). He also consulted, among others, Bligh's Narrative of the *Mutiny of the Bounty* (1790), and *A Narrative of the Honourable John Byron* (1768), by his grandfather the admiral, which describes 'the great distresses suffered by himself and his companions on the coast of Patagonia, from the year 1740, till their arrival in England, 1746'. Byron wrote to Murray (1821): 'I think that I told both you and Mr. Hobhouse, years ago, that [there] was not a *single circumstance* of it *not* taken from *fact*; not, indeed, from any *single* shipwreck, but all from *actual* facts of different wrecks.' The Variorum editors quote many parallel passages showing in what close detail Byron followed his sources.

XXVIII–XXXII. Details of the storm; the cutting away of the masts.

XXXIX–XLIII. Further details of their desperate plight.

LXIII. 6–7. *tertian Ague*: intermittent fever recurring every other day.

LXIV. 6. In classical mythology the three Parcae or Fates controlled the birth, life, and death of men. Clotho held the distaff, Lachesis spun the thread of life, and Atropos severed it.

LXV. 8. *troublesome to pay*: as an undergraduate Byron incurred debts with 'the tribe of Israel' amounting to more than £12,000.

LXVI. 8. *Argo*: the ship in which Jason sailed to Colchis on his quest for the Golden Fleece.

LXXV. 4. For stealing fire from heaven to give to man Prometheus was by the order of Zeus chained to a rock in the Caucasus; an eagle daily preyed on his liver, which was renewed by night.

LXXX–LXXXIII. The choice of another victim is meditated, but proves unnecessary.

LXXXIV. 8. Referring to the proverb, 'Truth lies at the bottom of a well.'

LXXXVI. 4. See the story of Lazarus and the rich man, *Luke*, 16. 19–26.

LXXXVII–XCV. Two fathers in the boat see their sons die, the one with apparent indifference, the other with anguish. A rainbow and a white bird bring hope to the survivors.

C. 8. *Candia*: in Crete.

CI. 3. In Greek mythology *Charon* ferries the dead across the River Styx to Hades.

CV. 8. *Leander* of Abydos used at night to swim across the Hellespont to visit Hero, a priestess of Aphrodite, at Sestos; on a stormy night he was drowned, and Hero threw herself into the sea. On 3 May 1810 Byron swam the Hellespont with Lieut. Ekenhead of the Marines. He often spoke with pride of this feat; see his poem *Written after Swimming from Sestos to Abydos*.

CX. 5. *jury-mast*: temporary mast used in an emergency.

CXIX. 3. *Irish lady*: The Variorum editors suggest that this was Lady Adelaide Forbes, whom Byron compared to the Apollo Belvedere.

CXX. 7. *basquina*: an outer skirt of dark material; *mantilla*: a shawl or wrap covering the head and shoulders.

CXXIII. 8. *Achilles* and Patroclus prepared a feast for Odysseus and Ajax and their attendants when they were sent by the Greek leaders to persuade Achilles to rejoin them in their war against Troy (*Iliad*, IX. 182 ff.).

CXXVII. 2. *Cyclades*: a group of Greek islands in the Aegean.

CXXIX. 7–8. 'I was a stranger, and ye took me in' (*Matthew*, 25. 35).

CXXX. 5. *'vous'*: (nous) Greek for sense, wit.

CXXXI. 8. Probably 1 *Corinthians*, 13. 13: 'And now abideth faith, hope, charity, these three; but the greatest of these is charity.' Cf. *Colossians*, 3. 14.

CXXXVII. 8. *A Narrative of the Honourable John Byron*. See note on XXIV–CIV.

CXLII. 4. *Aurora*: goddess of dawn.

CLIV–CLXVI. Haidée and Zoe give Juan food and clothing, and Haidée begins to teach him her language.

CLXIX. 7–8. In Roman mythology Ceres was the goddess of corn and agriculture, Bacchus the god of wine, Venus the goddess of love.

CLXX. 8. Neptune is the god of the sea, Pan of flocks and shepherds; Jove, or Jupiter, is the chief of the gods.

CLXXIV. 7. Zeus fell in love with Io and turned her into a heifer to conceal her from the jealousy of Hera; but Hera obtained the heifer from Zeus, and set Argos, who had eyes all over his body to guard her. Argos was killed by Hermes, whereupon Hera sent a gadfly to persecute Io, pursuing her from land to land. It is hard to see the force of Byron's reference; was he perhaps influenced by the need for a rhyme to Scio?

CLXXIX–CLXXX. A digression on the necessity of sometimes getting drunk and the pleasure of getting rid of the hang-over with hock and soda-water.

CXCVI–CCI. Description of Haidée's happiness in watching over Juan as he sleeps, and reflections on the treachery of men to women and its results.

CCV–CCXVI. Reflections on love and inconstancy (with reference to Juan's having forgotten Julia).

CANTO III

IV. 2. *planted*: abandoned (cf. French *planter là*).

VII–XI. Further reflections on the rarity of love in marriage which include the lines, 'Think you, if Laura had been Petrarch's wife,/He would have written sonnets all his life?'

XVI. 1–2. *Cape Matapan*: the southernmost point of the Peloponnese; the Mainots inhabit the mountainous regions nearby.

XX. 6. *careen*: lay a ship on its side for cleaning and repairs.

XXII–XXVI. The natural fears of husbands or fathers coming home after long absences ('Wives in their husbands' absences grow subtler,/And daughters sometimes run off with the butler'). Haidée's father, Lambro, approaches his house.

XXVIII. 3. According to the old Ptolemaic astronomy, the earth, at the centre of the universe, was surrounded by nine invisible spheres. The first seven carried the planets then known (Moon, Mercury, Venus, Sun, Mars, Jupiter, Saturn), the eighth the fixed stars; the ninth, the Crystalline Sphere, was supposed to account for the precession of the equinoxes. Revolving at different speeds, the spheres gave off sweet sounds which combined to form the music, or harmony, of the spheres.

XXIX. 6. *dervises*: fanatical followers of the Sudanese Mahdi in whose rites dancing and howling play an important part.

XXIX. 7. *Pyrrhic dance*: the famous war-dance of the Greeks, performed in armour to the flute.

XLII–LI. Lambro asks a reveller 'the meaning of this holiday', and is told that, the old master being dead, there is now a new master—'But certainly to one deem'd dead returning,/This revel seem'd a curious mode of mourning.' Unrecognized, he enters the house by a private way.

LVII. 7. 'It is too full of the milk of human kindness' (*Macbeth*, I. v. 17).

LVII. 8. The Cyclopes were giants living in Thrace; each had only one eye in the centre of the forehead. Ulysses and twelve of his crew were captured in Sicily by the Cyclops Polyphemus, who ate six of the crew; Ulysses blinded him, and escaped with the other six.

LVIII–LX. A digression on the violent anger of which a father is capable, and on family-feeling.

LXII. 5. The inhabitants of Sybaris, in south Italy, were proverbial for their love of luxury and their self-indulgence.

LXIV–LXVI. Description of the banqueting-hall, and mock-moralizing on the pleasures of the table.

LXX. 2. *jelick*: a vest or bodice worn by Turkish women.

LXX. 7. *baracan*: strictly, 'a sort of water-proof cloth of coarse wool or goat's hair', but loosely used by Byron (and other writers) for 'a fine cloth of silk or other delicate material'.

LXXIII. 7. *Zephyr*: the west wind, but used of any gentle wind.

LXXIV. 5. *Psyche*: a beautiful maiden loved by Cupid; united with him after many vicissitudes, she became a goddess.

LXXVI. 8. *King John*, IV. ii. 11.

LXXVII. 6. *aigrette*: a plume or tuft, usually of feathers.

LXXVIII. 2. *a poet*: much of Byron's description of this poet resembles his attacks on Southey in the Dedication and in other poems.

LXXVIII. 8. 'My heart is inditing a good matter' (*Psalm* 45. 1).

LXXIX–LXXXIII. Description of the poet as a 'turncoat' and a 'sad trimmer'.

LXXXV. 4. *Ça ira*: 'It will go'—the name of a popular patriotic song of the French Revolution with the refrain, 'Ah! ça ira, ça ira, ça ira,/Les aristocrates à la lanterne!'

LXXXV. 7. Several of Pindar's famous odes celebrated victors in horse-races or chariot-races in the Panhellenic Games.

LXXXVI. 6. 'Goethe pourroit représenter la littérature allemande toute entière' (Mme. de Staël, *De l'Allemagne*, I. 227).

LXXXVI. 7. '*Trecentisti*': the Italian poets of the fourteenth century, including Dante, Petrarch, and Boccaccio.

The Isles of Greece

1. ii. *Sappho*, one of the greatest Greek lyrical poets, lived on the island of Lesbos.

1. iv. *Delos*, the smallest of the Cyclades, was called out of the deep by the trident of Poseidon. It was the birthplace of Apollo and Artemis, and was consecrated to the worship of Apollo.

2. i. Scio (Chios) claimed to be the birthplace of Homer; Teos was the birthplace of Anacreon.

2. vi. '*Islands of the Blest*', or Fortunate Islands, an ancient name for the Canary Islands; used also of imaginary islands in faraway seas where peace and happiness reign.

3. i–vi. *Marathon*: the site, 22 miles from Athens, of the famous battle of 490 B.C. in which the Athenians under Miltiades defeated the Persians; the mound raised over the dead may still be seen.

4. i–vi. *Salamis*: an island not far from Athens off which, in 480 B.C., the Greeks destroyed the Persian fleet; the Persian king, Xerxes, is said to have watched the battle from a lofty mound on the shore.

7. vi. In 480 B.C. three hundred Spartans, under King Leonidas, for three days held up the vast land-army of Xerxes.

9. ii. The wine of Samos, an Aegean island, was celebrated.

9. vi. *Bacchanal*: drunken reveller.

10. ii. *phalanx*: a close-order formation of infantry; Pyrrhic here refers to the great Pyrrhus, King of Epirus (3rd cent. B.C.).

10. v. *Cadmus*, legendary founder of Thebes, is said to have introduced an alphabet into Greece.

11. iii–iv. *Anacreon* lived for many years in Samos under the patronage of Polycrates, its tyrant (or king).

12. iii. *Miltiades*, the victor of Marathon, was tyrant of the Thracian Chersonesus.

13. ii. *Suli*: on the Albanian border; *Parga*: in N. Greece.

13. iv–vi. *Doric mothers*: the Dorians, one of the great Hellenic races, were the first Greek settlers in the Peloponnese, which they are said to have conquered in conjunction with the Heraclidae, the descendants of Heracles.

14. i. *Franks*: originally the Teutonic nations which conquered Gaul in the 6th cent., but in the Levant sometimes used of the peoples of W. Europe; Lambro later refers to Juan as 'the Frank'. Byron may be thinking especially of the English, whose intervention in Continental affairs seemed to him to be influenced by mercenary motives; *Latin fraud* (l.v) may be an allusion to France.

16. i. *Sunium*, the promontory forming the southern tip of Attica, has upon it the ruins of a splendid temple of Poseidon.

XC. 5. Edmund Hoyle's *Short Treatise on Whist* (1742) was for more than a century the authoritative work on whist.

XC. 8. William Coxe, author of *Memoirs of John, Duke of Marlborough* (1818–19).

XCI. 6. *all the Nine*: the nine Muses.

XCI. 7–8. In his *Life of Milton* Dr. Johnson records that Milton was 'one of the last students in either University that suffered the publick indignity of corporal correction'. Johnson also reports the better-known fact that Milton's first wife, Mary Powell, returned to her parents not long after her marriage.

XCII. 3–5. In his *Lives of the Twelve Caesars* Suetonius refers to the wildness both of Caesar and of Titus in their youth. Burns, too, led an irregular life; an edition of his works (1800) contained a biography by Dr. James Currie. 'Cromwell's pranks' in his early days included the robbing of orchards.

XCIII. 1–8. '*Pantisocracy*': a project, planned in 1794, by Coleridge and Southey and other idealists, to establish on the banks of the Susquehanna a community in which all should have equal rights and powers, and in which human perfection might be attained; the project came to nothing. Byron often sneered at Wordsworth for accepting the sinecure of distributor of stamps for the County of Westmorland, and thus becoming 'excised' and 'hired' by the government; 'pedlar poems' is presumably an allusion to Wordsworth's poems about humble folk. Coleridge and Southey married sisters, Sarah and Edith Fricker, who were not, however, milliners.

xcv. 4. Joanna Southcott (1750–1814), a Devonshire farmer's daughter, was a religious fanatic. She wrote doggerel prophecies and claimed supernatural gifts. In 1802 she declared that she was about to be delivered of a spiritual being named Shiloh. She died of a brain disease; her followers numbered tens of thousands.

xcvi. 8. Ludovico Ariosto (1474–1533), author of the epic *Orlando Furioso*, was one of Byron's favourite poets.

xcvii. 4. *every Spring*: Southey was a very voluminous author, and published a substantial work almost every year in the first two decades of the century.

xcvii. 7. *epopée*: epic poetry.

xcviii. 1. 'Quandoque bonus dormitat Homerus' (*Ars Poetica*, 359).

xcviii. 4–8. Wordsworth's *The Waggoner* was published in 1819. For 'a boat' see *Peter Bell*, I. 1–4.

xcix. 3. *Charles's Wain*: a popular name for the Great Bear; the constellation has roughly the outline of a wheelbarrow or rustic wagon.

xcix. 4. At the end of Euripides's *Medea* Medea drives off with her children's corpses in a chariot drawn by dragons.

c. 5. In 1450 Jack Cade led a rebellion of common people against Henry VI and his council.

c. 8. Dryden's great political satire *Absalom and Achitophel* was published in 1681. The word 'sneer' perhaps refers to disparaging comments on a passage from Dryden's *The Indian Emperor* in Wordsworth's *Essay, Supplementary to the Preface*, in his *Poems* (1815).

cv. 5–7. Ravenna at one time had a great harbour, named Caesarea in honour of Augustus; later, when the Adriatic receded, the site of the harbour was planted with pine trees and orchards. For Byron this pine-forest 'breathes of the

Decameron', the famous collection of prose tales by Boccaccio; it is the scene of the story of Dryden's *Theodore and Honoria,* which is based on one of Boccaccio's tales.

CVI. 5–8. *spectre huntsman*: in *Theodore and Honoria,* Theodore, rejected by Honoria, causes her to see a vision of a woman pursued and pulled down by two mastiffs, which are urged on by a horseman on a black steed; she is thus cured of her haughtiness.

CVII. 1. *Hesperus*: the evening star.

CIX. 1–5. The Emperor Nero took his own life in 68 A.D. when a formidable revolt against his tyranny took place. Suetonius (*Lives of the Twelve Caesars*) records that, amidst the general rejoicing at his death, there were people who for a long time placed flowers upon his tomb.

CX. 6. '*wooden spoons*': at one time presented to the lowest on the honours list for the mathematical tripos at Cambridge.

CXI. 8. In the *Poetics* (Περὶ Ποιητικῆς) Aristotle discusses the structure of the epic.

CANTO IV

I. 5–8. Originally belonging to Venus as the morning star and Hesperus as the evening star, the name Lucifer ('light-bearer') was by the early Church Fathers, and by poets such as Milton, applied to Satan, 'hurl'd from heaven' for his sinful pride in aspiring to set himself up as the equal of God.

III. 5–6. 'My May of life/Is fall'n into the sere, the yellow leaf' (*Macbeth,* V. iii. 22–3).

IV. 5–8. *Lethe,* the river of forgetfulness, was one of the rivers of Hades; the souls of the dead had to drink of its waters in order to forget their mortal lives. Styx, the river of hate, flowed nine times round the infernal regions; the dead were ferried across it by Charon. Thetis dipped her son Achilles in the Styx to make him invulnerable; the heel by which she held him escaped the influence of the water, and this was the vulnerable point by which he was slain.

VI. 3. Luigi Pulci (1432–84) wrote the burlesque chivalric poem *Morgante Maggiore* the spirit of which Byron to some extent aimed at imitating in *Don Juan.*

VII. 7. *Apollo plucks me by the ear*: 'Cum canerem reges et praelia, Cynthius aurem/vellit et admonuit' (Virgil, *Eclogues,* VI. 3–4).

XII. 1. The saying goes back to classical times; it is used by Menander and Plautus.

L. 6. *galliots*: small, swift galleys using both sails and oars.

LII. 3. *Cassandra*: daughter of Priam of Troy, gifted with powers of prophecy.

LII. 6. *Bohea*: a type of China tea.

LIII. 2. A *naiad* is a nymph of a lake, fountain, or stream. *Phlegethon*, one of the rivers of Hades, flowed with liquid fire.

LIII. 5. *rack*: arrack, a spirit distilled from rice or molasses; here probably rum.

LVII. 8. *Simoom*: a hot, suffocating desert wind of Arabia and N. Africa.

LXI. 4–6. Byron is probably thinking of the Venus de' Medici, now in the Uffizi Gallery, Florence. Laocoon, a son of Priam, gave offence to Apollo, and was with his two sons crushed to death by serpents while sacrificing to Poseidon; the famous marble representing the three in their death agony was probably executed in the 2nd cent. B.C., and is now in the Vatican. The statue of the dying gladiator is in the Museum of the Capitol in Rome.

FURTHER READING

Editions

Steffan, Truman Guy, and Pratt, Willis W. (edd.). *Byron's 'Don Juan'*. 4 vols.: I, *The Making of a Masterpiece*; II, *A Variorum Edition*: *Cantos I–IV*; III, *A Variorum Edition*: *Cantos VI–XVII*; IV, *Notes on the Variorum Edition*. Texas U.P. and Nelson, 1957. The authoritative scholars' edition; records Byron's revisions, and prints the stanzas he wrote for Canto XVII; has a full introduction and notes.

Coleridge, Ernest Hartley, and Prothero, Rowland E. (edd.). *The Works of Lord Byron*. 13 vols. John Murray. 1898–1904. Vol. 6 contains *Don Juan*.

The complete *Don Juan* will be found in many other editions of Byron's poetical works, such as the Oxford Standard Authors edition.

Biography

Marchand, Leslie A. *Byron: A Biography*. 3 vols. John Murray. 1957. Of numerous biographical studies, this is the most up-to-date, comprehensive, and authoritative.

Nicolson, Harold. *Byron: The Last Journey, April 1823–April 1824*. Constable. 1924. A detailed account of Byron's last year.

Byron's *Letters and Journals* occupy Vols. 8–13 in *The Works of Lord Byron*, ed. Coleridge and Prothero (see above). An edition of his *Correspondence*, in 2 vols., was prepared in 1922 by Sir John Murray. Also of great interest is *Recollections of the Last Days of Shelley and Byron*, by E. J. Trelawny (1858), available in modern reprints.

Criticism

Arnold, Matthew. 'Byron', in *Essays in Criticism: Second Series* (1888), available in modern editions.

Grierson, H. J. C. *Poems of Lord Byron*. Chatto & Windus, 1923. A good selection with a stimulating critical introduction.

Bottrall, Ronald. 'Byron and the Colloquial Tradition in English Poetry', in *The Criterion XVIII* (1939). Interesting discussion which places Byron in the 'colloquial tradition' coming down through Chaucer, Donne, Dryden, and Pope.

Boyd, Elizabeth French. *Byron's Don Juan: A Critical Study*. Routledge & Kegan Paul, 1958 (first published in 1945). Excellent all-round study.

Ridenour, George M. *The Style of Don Juan*. Yale U.P., 1960. Detailed analysis.

Rutherford, Andrew. *Byron: A Critical Study*. Oliver & Boyd, 1961. Four sound chapters on *Don Juan*.

Auden, W. H. 'Don Juan', in *The Dyer's Hand and Other Essays*. Faber, 1963. Stimulating study by a poet who can himself be 'Byronic'.

Joseph, M. K., *Byron the Poet*. Gollancz, 1964. Nine Chapters on *Don Juan*.

Marchand, Leslie A. *Byron's Poetry: A Critical Introduction*. John Murray, 1965. Fairly full treatment of *Don Juan*, representing the most modern approaches.